THE PERSON WHO IS ME

Winnicott Studies Monograph Series

THE PERSON WHO IS ME
Contemporary Perspectives on the True and False Self

edited by
Val Richards

with
Gillian Wilce

London
KARNAC BOOKS
for
The Squiggle Foundation

"Ego Distortion in Terms of the True and False Self" by D. W. Winnicott reproduced by arrangement with Mark Paterson and Associates on behalf of the Winnicott Trust, London.

Excerpts:

From "The Waste Land" by T. S. Eliot, in *Collected Poems 1909–1962*, published by Faber & Faber, London, 1963; reproduced by permission.
From "Flash-Back" by James Greene, in *Dead Man's Fall*, published by Bodley Head, London, 1980; reproduced by permission.
From "The Voice" by Thomas Hardy, in *The Collected Poems*, published by Macmillan/Papermac, London, 1979; reproduced by permission.
From "Prayer before Birth" by Louis MacNeice, in *Collected Poems*, published by Faber & Faber, London, 1964; reproduced by permission.

First published in 1996 by
H. Karnac (Books) Ltd.
58 Gloucester Road
London SW7 4QY

British Library Cataloguing in Publication Data

A C.I.P. for this book is available from the British Library

ISBN 1 85575 130 5

Edited, designed, and produced by Communication Crafts

Printed by BPC Wheatons Ltd, Exeter
10 9 8 7 6 5 4 3 2 1

CONTENTS

ACKNOWLEDGEMENTS

The Editors wish to thank the following people for their valuable support and advice:

Editorial Committee: Jan Abram, Sheila Ernst, Nina Farhi, Gill Gregory, Wille Henriques, Rosie Parker, Margaret Walters, Lindsay Wells

Editorial Consultants: Gay Crace, Laurie Spurling

Administrator: Louise Exeter

The Trustees of The Squiggle Foundation

Karnac Books: Cesare Sacerdoti, Graham Sleight

CONTRIBUTORS

KATHERINE CAMERON is a psychoanalytic psychotherapist in private practice. She is a Member of the Institute of Psychotherapy and Social Studies and is currently completing the MA in Psychoanalysis at Middlesex University.

DR NINA COLTART is a psychoanalyst and was Director of the London Clinic of Psychoanalysis for ten years. Now retired after thirty-eight years in full-time practice, she is the author of *Slouching Towards Bethlehem* (1992), *How to Survive as a Psychotherapist* (1993), and *The Baby and the Bathwater*.

VAL RICHARDS is a psychoanalytic psychotherapist, the editor of *Winnicott Studies*, and on the staff of the Squiggle Foundation. She is a Member of the Institute of Psychotherapy and Social Studies and the Guild of Psychotherapists and teaches on various trainings. Her publications include "The Lac-king" in *Shakespeare and the Changing Curriculum* (1990), book reviews in the *British Journal of Psychotherapy*, and papers in *Winnicott Studies*.

FRANCES TUSTIN was an Honorary Member of the Association of Child Psychotherapists and an Honorary Affiliate of the British Psychoanalytical Society. Her publications include *Autistic States in Children* (1981), *Autistic Barriers in Neurotic Patients* (1986), and *The Protective Shell in Children and Adults* (1990).

DR KENNETH WRIGHT is a psychoanalyst and psychiatrist in private practice. He trained with the Independent Group of the British Psychoanalytical Society and at the Tavistock Clinic and Maudsley Hospitals. He is author of *Vision and Separation— Between Mother and Baby* (1991), which won the 1992 Mahler Literature Prize. He is particularly influenced by Winnicott, and his interests include the development and use of symbols and the relation between creativity and the life of the Self.

THE PERSON WHO IS ME

Introduction

Winnicott's radical paper, "Hate in the Countertransference" (1947), includes the much-quoted incident of his handling a disturbed and violent small boy in the care of himself and his wife. In order to contain the situation and his own violent feelings, he puts the child outside the house, saying: "What has happened has made me hate you." When the boy has calmed down, he can let himself in.

Successive groups of students, trainees, and particularly those working with children have expressed consternation, less at Winnicott's action, than at his words. Surely, as in the Christian precept, it is imperative to convey that one hates not the "sinner", but the "sin"? Yet here is Winnicott implying the inseparability of the child from its behaviour in their impact on Winnicott's own feelings. Would this not be unhelpful, even damaging? Possibly so—especially as the episode represents a strategy for Winnicott's own survival rather than some sacred prescription for treatment. What seems important, though, is that, instead of standing wholly outside the situation as the omnipotent adult, Winnicott demonstrates that he is right "in there" with the boy, who is given the satisfaction of hearing that HE, his very Self, not just his antics, has succeeded in getting through to Winnicott and acting on his feelings. And because of the procedures for recovery—that is, re-admission when he is ready—the boy hears simultaneously that Winnicott's hate for him is not fixed and implacable, but transient, fluid, reversible.

This incident serves as a touchstone, both for Winnicott's own notions of the Self and for those represented by the other contributors to this book. Firstly, it is a compressed enactment of Winnicott's belief that the surfaces of the Self, in infancy and in the process of psychotherapy, are shaped and modified by interaction and mirroring between the participants. Secondly, it is a salutary reminder of Winnicott's capacity as the acclaimed advocate of maternal "holding"—also for sharpness and for the sudden piercing stab of recognition. Behind such moments is Winnicott's ultimate description of the Self as "the person who is me".

Also portrayed in this non-clinical example is Winnicott's capacity to surrender, without being governed by theoretical preconceptions, to wherever a particular process may lead. This open experimental approach led to his understanding both of regression to dependence (as distinct from regression to earlier fixation points) and of silence, and to a tolerance of not understanding, with the vital if contentious recognition that not all sequences within a set time and special setting are necessarily meaningful. The possibilities of both nonsense and meaninglessness must be faced, without the sometimes distorting effect of inappropriate interpretations.

With his deep understanding of psychic mechanisms (as discussed here in chapter two, "Hunt the Slipper"), Winnicott's holistic view of the Self in health was of a "unit", quite distinct from his dichotomy between the tautological "True Self" and "False Self", which belongs to illness. Finally, he writes of a complex picture of the Self as composed of many parts, but simply expressed as "the person who is me" (Winnicott, 1970, p. 271). His comment that "a word like 'self' naturally knows more than we do; it uses us, and can command us" (Winnicott, 1960, p. 158) favours questioning above answering, mystery above certainty. It implies an element in the personality which, although sometimes equated with ego and id, as traditionally understood, transcends both of these, resembling the Jungian Self, the central organizing principle of the psyche, and paving the way for the notion of the transpersonal. It is notable that reviewing Winnicott's *Maturational Processes and The Facilitating Environment*, when first published in 1965, a Jungian reviewer wrote of both the overlap and the disparity:

> Winnicott insists that a young baby can be considered only in relation to its mother, and that psychologically they form a unit from which the baby gradually emerges as a separate individual, which he calls "unit status." This is close to Jung's view of the psychic interrelation of parents and children, but Winnicott puts the emergence from this relationship much earlier than Jung does, granting the healthy child a considerable degree of individuality by the end of the first year. [Fordham, 1967]

In a sense, Winnicott functions at the place where several ways meet, with nods in the direction not only of Jung, but of his own psychoanalytic inheritance. The impersonal Freudian drive model of superego, ego, and id rubs shoulders with Winnicott's more mystical notion of Self as the inviolate secret core of the personality, and with "objects" playing a more formative part.

For the Freudian infant, though, its "objects" were quite secondary to its instincts. As stated by Peter Fonagy, "For Freud, in infancy and early childhood, others in the external world are extensions of the Self" (Fonagy, 1995, p. 576). For the Kleinian infant, "objects" were sought from the outset, but also primarily for the service of instinct gratification. For Winnicott and other object-relations theorists, the need to relate took precedence over the desire for satisfaction. According to Fonagy, the "importance of an intersubjective union between infant and caregiver during the ages of nine to eighteen months [as researched by Stern et al.] . . . runs across most current psychoanalytic formulation". This perception that the infant "finds itself in the other" derives from dialectical theories of the Self and differs from classical psychoanalytical notions of internalization of objects in that "the infant internalizes the Self from the object on the basis of the object's capacity to represent the child as a thinking, feeling, intentional being" (ibid.).

Perhaps more than any other British practitioner, the late Frances Tustin, openly indebted to the ideas of Winnicott, has demonstrated the previously uncharted experience of the infant who fails to "find itself in the other", for whom severance from the womb/breast is a devastating severance from Self. In chapter four, "The Emergence of a Sense of Self", Tustin writes about "states that are so early that the sense of self is undeveloped", showing how work with autistic children enables us to "watch the early unfolding sense of Self and begin to realize the miracle of this achievement". As in much of Winnicott's own work, Tustin's discoveries about the arrested or sick Self "can throw light on an early infantile situation, and also on the difficulties encountered by some neurotic patients whose sense of personal identity is very insecure".

And, as indicated in the disparate chapters in this monograph, the concept of Self is elusive and supremely self-deconstructing. According to Christopher Bollas (quoted in chapter six by Nina Coltart):

> Self is an apparently indefinable, yet seemingly essential, word—it names its *thing*, it is saturated with *it*, the indescribable is signified. [Bollas, 1995, p. 148]

It is a kind of semantic free-for-all and, although "saturated with *it*", is also a bucket with a hole in it, an empty, never to be filled, signifier.

Winnicott's 1960 paper, "Ego Distortion in Terms of the True and False Self",[1] reprinted here as chapter one, therefore acts as an anchor for other less specific explorations. As Winnicott himself acknowledges, the concept has distinguished connections, including, most notably, R. D. Laing's *The Divided Self*, published in the same year as Winnicott's paper. Its antecedents in literature and philosophy are to be found both in popular fantasies of the "alter ego" or "doppelganger" and in the works of Conrad and Sartre. But, as argued in chapter two, "Hunt the Slipper", both the True/False concept and its implications, suffer the fate of becoming solidified and distorted in application.

---

[1] Published in *The Maturational Processes and the Facilitating Environment* (pp. 140–152). London: Hogarth Press, 1965 [reprinted London: Karnac Books, 1990].

The susceptibility to abuse of the True and False Self concept relates to Winnicott's literary style, which reflects a poetic, rather than a logical, relationship to experience, with theoretical innovations and clinical insights presented—enacted, rather—without great amplification or exposition. The deceptive simplicity of his imagery and aphorisms suggests links that can be more associative than rational. Often artfully (or artlessly) concealing their philosophical and psychoanalytical underpinning, they must be unpacked by the reader. Attempts to nail down in a definitive way the shifting connotations of such terms as "playing", "good-enough mother", and "mirroring"—which, like the Squiggle game itself, depend considerably on the reader's own interpretation—are risky. Hence the impossibility of a "Winnicottian School" of psychoanalysis, while it is also to be observed that in their highly diverse voyage around the Self, most contributors here are influenced by Winnicott's concept of mirroring, which thus functions as a unifying element to the collection.

Although differently elaborated, the mirroring metaphor reflects the earlier formulation of Lacan in 1936 and is mentioned in Winnicott's the "Mirror-Role of Mother and Family" (Winnicott, 1967). In chapter three, Katherine Cameron sheds light on the function of the mirror metaphor for Winnicott's and Lacan's views respectively of the Self/Subject. In placing the "meeting of the infant's need" above the "satisfaction of its instincts" through object relating and object usage (see chapter one), Winnicott is perhaps closer to the ideas of Lacan than either realized. For while Lacan exalts the "desire" of the subject for "recognition" above the satisfaction of her needs, each in his own way is concerned with how psychoanalytic treatment gets past the "fictions" of the presenting subject—in Winnicott's case, the False Self, the "nurse" who talks about the "patient"; and in Lacan's, the ego. Both, in effect, challenge the validity of the long-standing distinction between "need" and "desire".

In fact, the ideas shaping Winnicott's own view of the world, and the place and nature of the Self, are implicit rather than explicit. What is certain is the observation of Adam Phillips that "with blithe defiance Winnicott recreated, often beyond recognition, the work of everyone who influenced him" (Phillips, 1988, p. 5). This includes a strong infusion of nineteenth-century romanticism, where the innermost self emerges pristine, a child with an anguished soul and a mystical bond with the natural world, now viewed no longer as a clock set ticking by a distant deity, but as a dynamic process with an immanent divinity.

This aspect of the inner world of the Self is represented in chapter five, "Looking after the Self", by Ken Wright. Here the relationship between the Self, the world of nature with which it is interfused, and the interpersonal world of mother and infant are considered in the light of contemporary psychological research, prefigured by Winnicott.

From the mystical, it is a small step to the metaphysical, and for Nina Coltart (chapter six), the search for the Self, which extends beyond the frontiers of psychoanalysis, is informed by her own Buddhist conviction that in one sense there is no permanent single entity called Self, while in another sense we live and breathe by the opposite certainty of either its presence or its tantalizing absence. The psychoanalytic encounter is seen to mirror the precepts of Buddhism in its orchestrating, without pinning down, the diversity of Self experience. In such aphoristic clinical moments as Winnicott's "It was yourself that was searching" (1971c, p. 63), and "it is a joy to be hidden, but a disaster not to be found" (1963a, p. 186), there is an unwitting echo of Buddhism's more ludic formulations and the vision of Self as, above all, process.

This concept of process and Coltart's acknowledgement of Winnicott's "there is no such thing as a baby" (1952, p. 99) brings us back to the recognition that the arena of all Self experience is, for all its "splendid isolation", inexorably shared. The potential Self emerges through relationship of a particular kind, through engagement in the intermediate space between two or more participants, asserting, "We cannot speak ourselves". Coltart faces the painful as well as the positive implications of this, suggesting, finally, one might say, that "there is no such thing as a Self", in an enquiry that is saturated with selving.

Val Richards

CHAPTER ONE

Ego distortion
in terms of True and False Self

D. W. Winnicott

One recent development in psycho-analysis has been the increasing use of the concept of the False Self. This concept carries with it the idea of a True Self.

History

This concept is not in itself new. It appears in various guises in descriptive psychiatry and notably in certain religions and philosophical systems. Evidently a real clinical state exists which deserves study, and the concept presents psycho-analysis with an aetiological challenge. Psycho-analysis concerns itself with the questions:

(1) How does the False Self arise?
(2) What is its function?
(3) Why is the False Self exaggerated or emphasized in some cases?
(4) Why do some persons not develop a False Self system?

(5) What are the equivalents to the False Self in normal people?

(6) What is there that could be named a True Self?

It would appear to me that the idea of a False Self, which is an idea which our patients give us, can be discerned in the early formulations of Freud. In particular I link what I divide into a True and a False Self with Freud's division of the self into a part that is central and powered by the instincts (or by what Freud called sexuality, pregenital and genital), and a part that is turned outwards and is related to the world.

Personal contribution

My own contribution to this subject derives from my working at one and the same time

(a) as a paediatrician with mothers and infants and

(b) as a psycho-analyst whose practice includes a small series of borderline cases treated by analysis, but needing to experience in the transference a phase (or phases) of serious regression to dependence.

My experiences have led me to recognize that dependent or deeply regressed patients can teach the analyst more about early infancy than can be learned from direct observation of infants, and more than can be learned from contact with mothers who are involved with infants. At the same time, clinical contact with the normal and abnormal experiences of the infant–mother relationship influences the analyst's analytic theory since what happens in the transference (in the regressed phases of certain of his patients) is a form of infant–mother relationship.

I like to compare my position with that of Greenacre, who has also kept in touch with paediatrics while pursuing her practice of psycho-analysis. With her too it seems to be clear that each of the two experiences has influenced her in her assessment of the other experience.

Clinical experience in adult psychiatry can have the effect on a psycho-analyst of placing a gap between his assessment of a clinical state and his understanding of its aetiology. The gap derives from an impossibility of getting a reliable history of early infancy either from a psychotic patient or from the mother, or from more detached observers. Analytic patients who regress to serious dependence in the transference fill in this gap by showing their expectations and their needs in the dependent phases.

Ego-needs and id-needs

It must be emphasized that in referring to the meeting of infant needs I am not referring to the satisfaction of instincts. In the area that I am examining the instincts are not yet clearly defined as internal to the infant. The instincts can be as much external as can a clap of thunder or a hit. The infant's ego is building up strength and in consequence is getting towards a state in which id-demands will be felt as part of the self, and not as environmental. When this development occurs, then id-satisfaction becomes a very important strengthener of the ego, or of the True Self; but id-excitements can be traumatic when the ego is not yet able to include them, and not yet able to contain the risks involved and the frustrations experienced up to the point when id-satisfaction becomes a fact.

A patient said to me: "Good management" (ego care) "such as I have experienced during this hour *is* a feed" (id-satisfaction). He could not have said this the other way round, for if I had fed him he would have complied and this would have played into his False Self defence, or else he would have reacted and rejected my advances, maintaining his integrity by choosing frustration.

Other influences have been important for me, as for instance when periodically I have been asked for a note on a patient who is now under psychiatric care as an adult but who was observed by myself when an infant or small child. Often from my notes I have been able to see that the psychiatric state that now exists was already to be discerned in the infant–mother relationship. (I leave out infant–father relationships in this context because I am referring to early phenomena, those that concern the infant's relationship to the mother, or to the father as another mother. The father at this very early stage has not become significant as a male person.)

Example

The best example I can give is that of a middle-aged woman who had a very successful False Self but who had the feeling all her life that she had not started to exist, and that she had always been looking for a means of getting to her True Self. She still continues with her analysis, which has lasted many years. In the first phase of this research analysis (this lasted two or three years), I found I was dealing with what the patient called her "Caretaker Self". This "Caretaker Self":

(1) found psycho-analysis;

(2) came and sampled analysis, as a kind of elaborate test of the analyst's reliability;

(3) brought her to analysis;

(4) gradually after three years or more handed over its function to the analyst (this was the time of the depth of the regression, with a few weeks of a very high degree of dependence on the analyst);

(5) hovered round, resuming caretaking at times when the analyst failed (analyst's illness, analyst's holidays, etc.);

(6) its ultimate fate will be discussed later.

From the evolution of this case it was easy for me to see the defensive nature of the False Self. Its defensive function is to hide and protect the True Self, whatever that may be. Immediately it becomes possible to classify False Self organizations:

(1) At one extreme: the False Self sets up as real and it is this that observers tend to think is the real person. In living relationships, work relationships, and friendships, however, the False Self begins to fail. In situations in which what is expected is a whole person the False Self has some essential lacking. At this extreme the True Self is hidden.

(2) Less extreme: the False Self defends the True Self; the True Self is, however, acknowledged as a potential and is allowed a secret life. Here is the clearest example of clinical illness as an

organization with a positive aim, the preservation of the individual in spite of abnormal environmental conditions. This is an extension of the psycho-analytic concept of the value of symptoms to the sick person.

(3) More towards health: the False Self has as its main concern a search for conditions which will make it possible for the True Self to come into its own. If conditions cannot be found then there must be reorganized a new defence against exploitation of the True Self, and if there be doubt then the clinical result is suicide. Suicide in this context is the destruction of the total self in avoidance of annihilation of the True Self. When suicide is the only defence left against betrayal of the True Self, then it becomes the lot of the False Self to organize the suicide. This, of course, involves its own destruction, but at the same time eliminates the need for its continued existence, since its function is the protection of the True Self from insult.

(4) Still further towards health: the False Self is built on identifications (as for example that of the patient mentioned, whose childhood environment and whose actual nanny gave much colour to the False Self organization).

(5) In health: the False Self is represented by the whole organization of the polite and mannered social attitude, a "not wearing the heart on the sleeve", as might be said. Much has gone to the individual's ability to forgo omnipotence and the primary process in general, the gain being the place in society which can never be attained or maintained by the True Self alone.

So far I have kept within the bounds of clinical description. Even in this limited area recognition of the False Self is important, however. For instance, it is important that patients who are essentially False Personalities shall not be referred to students of psycho-analysis for analysis under a training scheme. The diagnosis of False Personality is here more important than the diagnosis of the patient according to accepted psychiatric classifications. Also in social work, where all types of case must be accepted and kept in treatment, this diagnosis of False Personality is important in the avoidance of extreme frustration associated with therapeutic failure in spite of seemingly sound social work based on analytic principles. Especially is this diagnosis important in the *selection* of students for training in psycho-analysis or in psychiatric social work, that is to say, in the selection of case-work students of all kinds. The organized False Self is associated with a rigidity of defences which prevents growth during the student period.

The mind and the False Self

A particular danger arises out of the not infrequent tie-up between the intellectual approach and the False Self. When a False Self becomes organized in an individual who has a high intellectual potential there is a very strong tendency for the mind to become the location of the False Self, and in this case there develops a dissociation between intellectual activity and psychosomatic existence. (In the healthy individual, it must be assumed, the mind is not something for the individual to exploit in escape from psychosomatic being. I have developed this theme at some length in "Mind and Its Relation to the Psyche-Soma", 1949a.)

When there has taken place this double abnormality, (i) the False Self organized to hide the True Self, and (ii) an attempt on the part of the individual to solve the personal problem by the use of a fine intellect, a clinical picture results which is peculiar in that it very easily deceives. The world may observe academic success of a high degree, and may find it hard to believe in the very real distress of the individual concerned, who feels "phoney" the more he or she is successful. When such individuals destroy themselves in one way or another, instead of fulfilling promise, this invariably produces a sense of shock in those who have developed high hopes of the individual.

Aetiology

The main way in which these concepts become of interest to psycho-analysts derives from a study of the way a False Self develops at the beginning, in the infant–mother relationship, and (more important) the way in which a False Self does not become a signifi-cant feature in normal development.

The theory relative to this important stage in ontogenetic devel-opment belongs to the observation of infant-to-mother (regressed patient-to-analyst) living, and it does not belong to the theory of early mechanisms of ego-defence organized against id-impulse, though of course these two subjects overlap.

To get to a statement of the relevant developmental process it is essential to take into account the mother's behaviour and atti-tude, because in this field dependence is real, and near absolute. *It is not possible to state what takes place by reference to the infant alone.*

In seeking the aetiology of the False Self we are examining the stage of first object-relationships. At this stage the infant is most of the time unintegrated, and never fully integrated; cohesion of the various sensori-motor elements belongs to the fact that the mother holds the infant, sometimes physically, and all the time figura-tively. Periodically the infant's gesture gives expression to a spontaneous impulse; the source of the gesture is the True Self, and the gesture indicates the existence of a potential True Self. We need to examine the way the mother meets this infantile omnipo-tence revealed in a gesture (or a sensori-motor grouping). I have here linked the idea of a True Self with the spontaneous gesture. Fusion of the motility and erotic elements is in process of becom-ing a fact at this period of development of the individual.

The mother's part

It is necessary to examine the part played by the mother, and in doing so I find it convenient to compare two extremes; by one extreme the mother *is a good-enough mother* and by the other the mother *is not a good-enough mother*. The question will be asked: what is meant by the term "good-enough"?

The good-enough mother meets the omnipotence of the infant and to some extent makes sense of it. She does this repeatedly. A True Self begins to have life, through the strength given to the infant's weak ego by the mother's implementation of the infant's omnipotent expressions.

The mother who is not good enough is not able to implement the infant's omnipotence, and so she repeatedly fails to meet the infant gesture; instead she substitutes her own gesture which is to be given sense by the compliance of the infant. This compliance on the part of the infant is the earliest stage of the False Self, and belongs to the mother's inability to sense her infant's needs.

It is an essential part of my theory that the True Self does not become a living reality except as a result of the mother's repeated success in meeting the infant's spontaneous gesture or sensory hallucination. (This idea is closely linked with Sechehaye's [1951] idea contained in the term "symbolic realization". This term has played an important part in modern psycho-analytic theory, but it is not quite accurate since it is the infant's *gesture or hallucination* that is made real, and the capacity of the infant *to use a symbol* is the result.)

There are now two possible lines of development in the scheme of events according to my formulation. *In the first case* the mother's adaptation *is good enough* and in consequence the infant begins to believe in external reality which appears and behaves as by magic (because of the mother's relatively successful adaptation to the infant's gestures and needs), and which acts in a way that does not clash with the infant's omnipotence. On this basis the infant can gradually abrogate omnipotence. The True Self has a spontaneity, and this has been joined up with the world's events. The infant can now begin to enjoy the *illusion* of omnipotent creating and controlling, and then can gradually come to recognize the illusory element, the fact of playing and imagining. Here is the basis for the symbol which at first is *both* the infant's spontaneity or hallucination, *and also* the external object created and ultimately cathected.

In between the infant and the object is some thing, or some activity or sensation. In so far as this joins the infant to the object (viz. maternal part-object), so far is this the basis of symbol-formation. On the other hand, in so far as this something separates instead of joins, so is its function of leading on to symbol-formation blocked.

In the second case, which belongs more particularly to the subject under discussion, the mother's adaptation to the infant's hallucinations and spontaneous impulses is deficient, *not good enough*. The process that leads to the capacity for symbol-usage does not get started (or else it becomes broken up, with a corresponding withdrawal on the part of the infant from advantages gained).

When the mother's adaptation is not good enough at the start the infant might be expected to die physically, because cathexis of external objects is not initiated. The infant remains isolated. But in practice the infant lives, but lives falsely. The protest against being forced into a false existence can be detected from the earliest stages. The clinical picture is one of general irritability, and of feeding and other function disturbances which may, however, disappear clinically, only to reappear in serious form at a later stage.

In this second case, where the mother cannot adapt well enough, the infant gets seduced into a compliance, and a compliant False Self reacts to environmental demands and the infant seems to accept them. Through this False Self the infant builds up a false set of relationships, and by means of introjections even attains a show of being real, so that the child may grow to be just like mother, nurse, aunt, brother, or whoever at the time dominates the scene. The False Self has one positive and very important function: to hide the True Self, which it does by compliance with environmental demands.

In the extreme examples of False Self development, the True Self is so well hidden that spontaneity is not a feature in the infant's living experiences. Compliance is then the main feature, with imitation as a speciality. When the degree of the split in the infant's person is not too great there may be some almost personal living through imitation, and it may even be possible for the child to act a special role, that of the True Self *as it would be if it had had existence.*

In this way it is possible to trace the point of origin of the False Self, which can now be seen to be a defence, a defence against that which is unthinkable, the exploitation of the True Self, which would result in its annihilation. (If the True Self ever gets exploited and annihilated this belongs to the life of an infant whose mother was not only "not good enough" in the sense set out above, but was good and bad in a tantalizingly irregular manner. The mother here has as part of her illness a need to cause and to maintain a muddle in those who are in contact with her. This may appear in a transference situation in which the patient tries to make the analyst mad: Bion, 1959; Searles, 1959. There may be a degree of this which can destroy the last vestiges of an infant's capacity to defend the True Self.)

I have attempted to develop the theme of the part the mother plays in my paper on "Primary Maternal Preoccupation" (1956). The assumption made by me in this paper is that, in health, the mother who becomes pregnant gradually achieves a high degree of identification with her infant. This develops during the pregnancy, is at its height at the time of lying in, and it gradually ceases in the weeks and months after the confinement. This healthy thing that happens to mothers has both hypochondriacal and secondary narcissistic implications. This special orientation on the part of the mother to her infant not only depends on her own mental health, but also it is affected by the environment. In the simplest case the man, supported by a social attitude which is itself a development from the man's natural function, deals with external reality for the woman, and so makes it safe and sensible for her to be temporarily in-turned, self-centred. A diagram of this resembles the diagram of an ill paranoid person or family. (One is reminded here of Freud's, 1920, description of the living vesicle with its receptive cortical layer. . . .)

The development of this theme does not belong here, but it is important that the function of the mother should be understood. This function is by no means a recent development, belonging to civilization or to sophistication or to intellectual understand-ing. No theory is acceptable that does not allow for the fact that mothers have always performed this essential function well enough. This essential maternal function enables the mother to know about her infant's earliest expectations and needs, and makes her personally satisfied in so far as the infant is at ease. It is because of this identification with her infant that she knows how to hold her infant, so that the infant starts by existing and not by reacting. Here is the origin of the True Self which cannot become a reality without the mother's specialized relationship, one which might be described by a common word: devotion.[1]

---

[1] On account of this I called my series of talks to mothers, "The Ordinary Devoted Mother and Her Baby" (Winnicott, 1949b).

The True Self

The concept of "A False Self" needs to be balanced by a formulation of that which could properly be called the True Self. At the earliest stage the True Self is the theoretical position from which come the spontaneous gesture and the personal idea. The spontaneous gesture is the True Self in action. Only the True Self can be creative and only the True Self can feel real. Whereas a True Self feels real, the existence of a False Self results in a feeling unreal or a sense of futility.

The False Self, if successful in its function, hides the True Self, or else finds a way of enabling the True Self to start to live. Such an outcome may be achieved by all manner of means, but we observe most closely those instances in which the sense of things being real or worth while arrives during a treatment. My patient to whose case I have referred has come near the end of a long analysis *to the beginning of her life.* She contains no true experience, she has no past. She starts with fifty years of wasted life, but at last she feels real, and therefore she now wants to live.

The True Self comes from the aliveness of the body tissues and the working of body-functions, including the heart's action and breathing. It is closely linked with the idea of the Primary Process, and is, at the beginning, essentially not reactive to external stimuli, but primary. There is but little point in formulating a True Self idea except for the purpose of trying to understand the False Self, because it does no more than collect together the details of the experience of aliveness.

Gradually the degree of sophistication of the infant becomes such that it is more true to say that the False Self hides the infant's inner reality than to say that it hides the True Self. By this time the infant has an established limiting membrane, has an inside and an outside, and has become to a considerable extent disentangled from maternal care.

It is important to note that according to the theory being formulated here the concept of an individual inner reality of objects applies to a stage later than does the concept of what is being termed the True Self. The True Self appears as soon as there is any mental organization of the individual at all, and it means little more than the summation of sensori-motor aliveness.

The True Self quickly develops complexity, and relates to external reality by natural processes, by such processes as develop in the individual infant in the course of time. The infant then comes to be able to react to a stimulus without trauma because the stimulus has a counterpart in the individual's inner, psychic reality. The infant then accounts for all stimuli as projections, but this is a stage that is not necessarily achieved, or that is only partially achieved, or it may be reached and lost. This stage having been achieved, the infant is now able to retain the sense of omnipotence even when reacting to environmental factors that the observer can discern as truly external to the infant. All this precedes by years the infant's capacity to allow in intellectual reasoning for the operation of pure chance.

Every new period of living in which the True Self has not been seriously interrupted results in a strengthening of the sense of being real, and with this goes a growing capacity on the part of the infant to tolerate two sets of phenomena: These are:

(1) Breaks in continuity of True Self living. (Here can be seen a way in which the birth process might be traumatic, as for instance when there is delay without unconsciousness.)

(2) Reactive or False Self experiences, related to the environment on a basis of compliance. This becomes the part of the infant which can be (before the first birthday) taught to say "Ta", or, in other words, can be taught to acknowledge the existence of an environment that is becoming intellectually accepted. Feelings of gratitude may or may not follow.

The normal equivalent of the False Self

In this way, by natural processes, the infant develops an ego-organization that is adapted to the environment; but this does not happen automatically and indeed it can only happen if first the True Self (as I call it) has become a living reality, because of the mother's good-enough adaptation to the infant's living needs. There is a compliant aspect to the True Self in healthy living, an ability of the infant to comply and not to be exposed. The ability to compromise is an achievement. The equivalent of the False Self in normal development is that which can develop in the child into a social manner, something which is adaptable. In health this social manner represents a compromise. At the same time, in health, the compromise ceases to become allowable when the issues become crucial. When this happens the True Self is able to override the compliant self. Clinically this constitutes a recurring problem of adolescence.

Degrees of False Self

If the description of these two extremes and their aetiology is accepted it is not difficult for us to allow in our clinical work for the existence of a low or a high degree of the False Self defence, ranging from the healthy polite aspect of the self to the truly split-off compliant False Self which is mistaken for the whole child. It can easily be seen that sometimes this False Self defence can form the basis for a kind of sublimation, as when a child grows up to be an actor. In regard to actors, there are those who can be themselves and who also can act, whereas there are others who can only act, and who are completely at a loss when not in a role, and when not being appreciated or applauded (acknowledged as existing).

In the healthy individual who has a compliant aspect of the self but who exists and who is a creative and spontaneous being, there is at the same time a capacity for the use of symbols. In other words health here is closely bound up with the capacity of the individual to live in an area that is intermediate between the dream and the reality, that which is called the cultural life. (See "Transitional Objects and Transitional Phenomena", 1951.) By contrast, where there is a high degree of split between the True Self and the False Self which hides the True Self, there is found a poor capacity for using symbols, and a poverty of cultural living. Instead of cultural pursuits one observes in such persons extreme restlessness, an inability to concentrate, and a need to collect impingements from external reality so that the living-time of the individual can be filled by reactions to these impingements.

Clinical application

Reference has already been made to the importance of a recognition of the False Self personality when a diagnosis is being made for the purposes of the assessment of a case for treatment, or the assessment of a candidate for psychiatric or social psychiatric work.

Consequences for the psycho-analyst

If these considerations prove to have value, then the practising psycho-analyst must be affected in the following ways:

(a) In analysis of a False Personality the fact must be recognized that the analyst can only talk to the False Self of the patient about the patient's True Self. It is as if a nurse brings a child, and at first the analyst discusses the child's problem, and the child is not directly contacted. Analysis does not start until the nurse has left the child with the analyst, and the child has become able to remain alone with the analyst and has started to play.

(b) At the point of transition, when the analyst begins to get into contact with the patient's True Self, there must be a period of extreme dependence. Often this is missed in analytic practice. The patient has an illness, or in some other way gives the analyst a chance to take over the False Self (nursemaid) function, but the analyst at that point fails to see what is happening, and in consequence it is others who care for the patient and on whom the patient becomes dependent in a period of disguised regression to dependence, and the opportunity is missed.

(c) Analysts who are not prepared to go and meet the heavy needs of patients who become dependent in this way must be careful so to choose their cases that they do not include False Self types.

In psycho-analytic work it is possible to see analyses going on indefinitely because they are done on the basis of work with the False Self. In one case, a man patient who had had a considerable amount of analysis before coming to me, my work really started with him when I made it clear to him that I recognized his non-existence. He made the remark that over the years all the good work done with him had been futile because it had been done on the basis that he existed, whereas he had only existed falsely. When I had said that I recognized his non-existence he felt that he had been communicated with for the first time. What he meant was that his True Self that had been hidden away from infancy had now been in communication with his analyst in the only way which was not dangerous. This is typical of the way in which this concept affects psycho-analytic work.

I have referred to some other aspects of this clinical problem. For instance, in "Withdrawal and Regression" (1954) I traced in the treatment of a man the evolution in the transference of my contact with (his version of) a False Self, through my first contact with his True Self, to an analysis of a straightforward kind. In this case withdrawal had to be converted into regression as described in the paper.

A principle might be enunciated, that in the False Self area of our analytic practice we find we make more headway by recognition of the patient's non-existence than by a long-continued working with the patient on the basis of ego-defence mechanisms. The patient's False Self can collaborate indefinitely with the analyst in the analysis of defences, being so to speak on the analyst's side in the game. This unrewarding work is only cut short profitably when the analyst can point to and specify an absence of some essential feature: "You have no mouth", "You have not started to exist yet", "Physically you are a man, but you do not know from experience anything about masculinity", and so on. These recognitions of important fact, made clear at the right moments, pave the way for communication with the True Self. A patient who had had much futile analysis on the basis of a False Self, co-operating vigorously with an analyst who thought this was his whole self, said to me: "The only time I felt hope was when you told me that you could see no hope, and you continued with the analysis."

On the basis of this one could say that the False Self (like the multiple projections at later stages of development) deceives the analyst if the latter fails to notice that, regarded as a whole functioning person, the False Self, however well set up, lacks something, and that something is the essential central element of creative originality.

Many other aspects of the application of this concept will be described in the course of time, and it may be that in some ways the concept itself will need to be modified. My object in giving an account of this part of my work (which links with the work of other analysts) is that I hold the view that this modern concept of the False Self hiding the True Self *along with the theory of its aetiology* is able to have an important effect on psycho-analytic work. As far as I can see it involves no important change in basic theory.

CHAPTER TWO

Hunt the slipper

Val Richards

In this discussion, I attempt to show the risks inherent in according both theoretical status and clinical application to Winnicott's creative, essentially poetic perception of psychic disturbance in terms of a "split" into "True" and "False" "Self". This model of "ego distortion" is compared with Winnicott's more pluralistic view of the Self, as expressed in one of his last papers (Winnicott, 1970, p. 271). There he prefers the terms "dissociation" and "parts of the Self", with a finally tentative depiction of the Self in sickness and in health, which excludes reference to either "True" or "False", and refers to the Self as the "Person who is me".

For Winnicott, in his 1960 paper (chapter one herein), the notion of "True" is conjured up primarily as a means of conceptualizing "False". In acknowledging that he is not the author of the concept, he mentions its strong historical and contemporary precedents which tend to focus on the "False" element, with the attendant need to conceptualize "True".

The healthy, undamaged personality is elsewhere referred to by Winnicott less as a "True" Self than as a "unit" Self. Thus, the articulation of a "split" between "True" and "False" Self is born of pathology, of psychic disturbance. Just as only those struggling for breath are aware of breathing, and only those who feel "unreal" long to feel "real", so it is those who feel themselves, or are seen to have, a False Self who dream of an imagined True Self.

The term "False" is complicated in several ways not least because Winnicott's own explorations are at times muddled and contradictory. Firstly, there is his attempt to align his True/False model with Freud's "division of the self into a part that is central and powered by the instincts [id] . . . and a part that is turned outwards and is related to the world [ego]" (p. 8 herein), as if "id" is more "true" than "ego". Yet this is followed later by Winnicott's contradictory claim that "id-satisfaction becomes *a very important strengthener of the ego, or of the True Self*" (p. 9; my italics). Thus the True Self is now equated with the ego. Indeed, the whole weight of his thought in relation to early development tends towards the supremacy of ego and ego-relatedness. Not surprisingly, this initial attempt at calibration with Freud's model of the Self is dropped, with the slightly impatient comment that

> The True Self comes from the aliveness of the body tissues and the working of body-functions, including the heart's action and breathing. It is closely linked with the idea of the Primary Process, and is, at the beginning, essentially not reactive to external stimuli, but primary. There is but little point in formulating a True Self idea except for the purpose of trying to understand the False Self, because it does no more than collect together the details of the experience of aliveness. [p. 17]

The "False" perspective is further complicated by its intrinsically pejorative connotations, which, however, do not prevent Winnicott from stretching the notion of "False Self organization", in his theoretical account, to encompass five degrees or states which move successively further towards *health*. From the most extreme state of the subject's being totally severed from her True Self; to a more hopeful secret nurturing of the True by the False; to the False more actively seeking conditions for the realization of the True; to the viable identifications of the False with benign real-life figures, Winnicott traces the False Self to its final position. Here, it is little more or less than an essential social mask, akin to Jung's "persona". In this last form, it is, therefore, neither truly False nor involuntarily forced at the earliest developmental stage. Yet both extreme sickness and relative health are comprehended in the appellation "False".

These distinctions are, states Winnicott, based on *clinical* description, and he includes illustrations of patients who felt they had not yet existed, who lived solely through their intellects, who did not feel real, of actors who were animated only by their roles. It seems that essential for therapeutic progress was an eventual piercing of the patient's unconscious façade, with such points as, "You have no mouth", "You have not started to exist yet".

Thus, the metaphor of a True/False split actually issued from conscious lived moments between Winnicott and his patients, as "an idea which our patients give us". Winnicott is, therefore, concerned to distinguish between his devised *aetiology* of the False Self—which refers primarily to its persistent unconscious levels of functioning—and the more conscious manifestations, readily identified by both patient and therapist together as a False Self defence. The patients involved are usually "deeply regressed", "borderline" patients, who need a period of "extreme dependence" and whose primary concern is to recover the roots of their being.

This gap between pragmatically observed False Self manifestations and Winnicott's proposed aetiology is notable in that the subtle intricacies and interplay of an adult's functioning are then ascribed by him to a single dominant cause. For Winnicott proposes that the False Self arises at the most plastic early stage when the infant resembles melted sealing wax in its susceptibility to its mother's inscriptions. The impulses that generate the spontaneous gesture of the nascent (in this context, "True") Self towards and in relation to M/Other, if obstructed by her failure in empathy or through impingement, lead to the formation of a False (also Caretaker) Self for the protection of the True:

> It is not possible to state what takes place by reference to the infant
> alone. . . . The mother who is not good enough is not able to
> implement her infant's omnipotence, and so she repeatedly
> fails to meet the infant gesture; instead she substitutes her
> own gesture which is to be given sense by the compliance of
> the infant. This compliance on the part of the infant is the

earliest stage of the False Self, and belongs to the mother's
inability to sense her infant's needs. [p. 14; italics in original]

This obstruction to healthy development relates to Winnicott's
powerful mirroring metaphor, most fully elaborated in "The
Mirror-Role of Mother . . ." (Winnicott, 1967), an inspired representation of earliest mother/infant interactions and holding,
which heralds the findings of such contemporary researchers as
Brazelton, Stern, and Trevarthen (cf. Ken Wright, chapter five).
The poorly reflected infant is presented by Winnicott as the invol-
untary casualty of its mother's depression and other defects,
which become, as it were, clamped upon the baby. This is also
referred to as the mother's inadequate adaptation to the infant's
hallucinations and spontaneous impulses.

The sense that the mother's depressive withdrawal and
deadness play such a major part in the formation of the False Self
derives not only from Winnicott's own observation and engagement with thousands of mothers and babies, but from the fact that
"deeply regressed patients can teach the analyst more about early
infancy than can be learned from direct observation of infants and
more than can be learned from mothers who are involved with
infants" (p. 8 herein). Also, Winnicott's own childhood experience
appears to have played a part in shaping his theory, as expressed
in the poem he presented to a colleague not long before his death:

> Mother below is weeping
> > weeping
> > weeping
> Thus I knew her
> Once, stretched out on her lap
> > as now on dead tree
> I learned to make her smile
> > to stem her tears
> > to undo her guilt
> > to cure her inward death
> To enliven her was my living.
> > [Phillips, 1988, p. 29]

The juxtaposition of these two concepts—"good-enough" and
"not good-enough" maternal mirroring/adaptation, and the True/
False split—points to the great weight laid upon the single aetio-

logical factor of defective mothering. Notwithstanding our own urges to establish clear causes and original "blame" for present disorders, Winnicott's implicit suppression of other possible factors in the formation of the False Self appears as a gigantic leap from B to A, from "mirroring" to "splitting". For surely, it can never be known with that kind of certainty that the complexity and twists of a mature personality stem from a single environmental root. Apart from constitutional elements, it is at least possible that a False Self personality evolves as a result of later trauma (as, for example, proposed in the work of Kohut).

Thus, for reasons that will emerge further, there are risks in the process whereby a description that started life as an apt recognition of a particular psychic state turns into a diagnostic category, which can issue in such dicta as Winnicott's influential remark, "You cannot analyse the False Self". For, however valuable as a tip to novices, such a precept lends substance to the impression of the False and the True Self as two discrete entities. It can encourage the seductive idea that one's mode of being, one's self presentation and behaviour with another or others, is in some way unrepresentative, "False" or phoney. It can be a way of disowning what is disliked about one's behaviour in the consoling knowledge of one's hidden "True Self". Although the True/False lens frequently seems to make sense of clinical experience, this can be at the cost of distortion and oversimplification. The game of Hunt the Slipper(y) Self gets played enthusiastically by therapist and patient alike, whose equally vital surface behaviour and concerns might then be marginalized by both participants.

This tendency is, I suggest, reinforced by the intrinsic fixity of the image of a True/False dichotomy, suggesting that behind, beneath, or beyond the "falsity" of the manifest expression is something more "True", because more "deep". It promotes this picture of the Self in two distinct layers, one above the other, or one surrounding the other, like a fortress or carapace protecting the poor snail/Self within. It also suggests a rather static state of affairs "in there", quite at odds both with Winnicott's (Kleinian) vision of drama between internal objects and with his radical theory of potential space between participants as the theatre where individual Self development takes place. The idea of a discrete False Self/True Self entity negates the vision that I believe is promoted by Winnicott's concept of the transitional. This is the vision of infant and mother/patient and therapist as uniquely compositions of one another, so that he who departs at the end of a session dissolves, to reform and resume other roles and faces for other people and places. For I suggest that the False Self, especially when functioning as a more or less healthy social mask, is not so much a consistent attribute as, like other psychic states, more a fluid to-ing and fro-ing, even within a single session, a "here today with me, gone tomorrow with you". Perhaps also it is important to bear in mind Winnicott's rather dark view of the individual as an isolate, "permanently non-communicating, permanently unknown, in fact unfound" (1963a, p. 187).

Possibly, even, the mere assumption that an individual (patient) "possesses" a False Self structure independent of the other's (or analyst's) own personality may directly contribute to a False Self manifestation in the patient; Winnicott's compelling evocation of the experience of working with a "False Personality" illustrates this tendency:

> In analysis of a False Personality the fact must be recognized that the analyst can only talk to the False Self of the patient about the patient's True Self. It is as if a nurse brings a child, and at first the analyst discusses the child's problem, and the child is not directly contacted. Analysis does not start until the nurse has left the child with the analyst, and the child has become able to remain alone with the analyst and has started to play. [p. 20 herein]

This analogy further supports the vision of a two-tier structure to the personality, while a clearly differentiated two-stage process to the psychoanalysis of a "False Personality" fosters an attitude, prevalent in both analytic and humanistic work, that the main quarry, the real prize of the "enter-prize", is the patient's direct expression of naked emotion by the "child within". The metaphorical status of Winnicott's "child" is, however, here unmistakable and related to his theory of "playing", which epitomizes the liberation of the unconscious, the Self, and free association within the analytic relationship. Yet it is not uncommon for such a "child" to be referred to as a literal entity. Furthermore, and more integral to this composite image of nurse/patient, the implicit discrimination between the value/realness of the "nurse"/patient's contribution in talking *about* herself and the "child"/patient's *directly expressing* herself suggests that the first level of communication is a mere preliminary to the fuller, more real mode, implying, however unintentionally, that, once gone, the "nurse" is gone for good, and, once here, the "child" has come to stay.

Arising from its own context, again Winnicott's metaphor is an inspired insight, but as a therapeutic prescription to others it is potentially damaging. In the apparent straitjacketing of treatment into two such clearly distinct stages, like the True/False metaphor, is an inducement to undervalue the patient's less emotionally charged "talking about" herself. Regarding this as a False Self defence, there might then follow an attempt to push the patient into greater feats of "Self" expression, to reach the kernel of the nut, the pearl in the oyster. Such an attitude is likely to widen further the very gap between thought and feeling, which analysis seeks to integrate.

This question of the analyst's influence on the patient relates to the key constituent of Winnicott's False Self formulation: compliance, which is seen as the fundamental stance of the infant who develops a False Self as the means of warding off impingements to the True Self: "This compliance on the part of the infant is the earliest stage of the False Self, and belongs to the mother's inability to sense her infant's needs" (p. 14).

Compliance, then, is viewed by Winnicott as the essential re-active adaptation to an ill-matched or impinging mother. Yet in the transference, compliance tends to be regarded as belonging wholly to the *patient* and the patient's past, rather than possibly also to an ill-matched or impinging *therapist*. Regarded as adverse, as imitative, as inappropriately placatory, compliance is seen as the antithesis of the spontaneous agency that derives from the True Self. Thus, Winnicott's crucial implication that compliance might also belong to the *analyst's* inability to sense his *patient's* needs is easily suppressed.

For this issue of compliance reflects another anomaly of the analytic encounter and the difficulty of sustaining both the ideal of "playing together" and analytic detachment, with its sometimes bewildering mixture of "withness" and "aboveness". The original myth of analytic neutrality has gained such a hold on popular and professional imagination that it is possible for both participants in analytic work to avoid the realization that a neutral analyst would be toneless and unanimated—a dead analyst, a computer—and to blind themselves to the value-laden nature of the alive analyst's responses and silences.

Thanks to the basic asymmetry of the relationship, with the patient as the primarily vulnerable and self-revealing member of the dyad, the power usually projected onto the analyst tends to insert the patient into the position of pupil, of petitioner, with the analyst's very presence situating him in the transference as "teacher", in addition to all the other alternating and composite figures. The patient longs to be a good (or the obverse of compliant, bad) pupil/patient. And such desires are important allies in the fostering of the therapy, so that, within such an unconscious pupil/teacher dynamic, the unspoken message is transmitted, or imagined, that compliance is really "good".

This can cause every utterance and every silence of the therapist to be experienced, unconsciously, by the patient as a lesson to be absorbed, so that too relentless an overt analysis of the compliant child/pupil impulse could be tantamount to the analyst's *sending* the "nurse" away, instead of waiting for her to leave as in Winnicott's description. This might lead to the patient's mystification, causing the False Self carapace to harden, instead of cracking, as the patient falls into the equally compliant trap expressed as: "My therapist conveys that compliance is bad. Therefore, I must avoid compliance and *learn* to be spontaneous and autonomous." It might, therefore, be useful to distinguish between the reactive compliance that, for Winnicott, forms the main False Self defence and some degree of what might be called "healthy" compliance, which can be equally unconscious and may be endemic to the analytic situation. Indeed, such a distinction is supported by Winnicott's own comment that "there is a compliant aspect to the true Self in healthy living, an ability of the infant to comply and not be exposed. The ability to compromise is an achievement" (pp. 18–19).

The risks and limitations inherent in transposing original insights to wider clinical practice are suggested in the following case material, in which the metaphor of the True/False Self split infiltrated the therapy, resulting in both distortion and oversimplification. This example illustrates also the function of compliance and the presence of a hidden teacher/pupil dynamic.

Peter, the director of a successful firm, felt crippled because of intolerable pressure from work and family and because he had always bottled up everything and never expressed any feelings, nor talked about himself to anyone. Placatory and compliant with wife, children, and employees, he voiced the feeling of living falsely and a desire to discover what he referred to as his "Real Self".

In the ensuing sessions, however, it was as if Peter faithfully exemplified Winnicott's evocation, discussed above, of the nurse bringing the child and talking *about* its problems with the analyst. For Peter was soon recounting vast improvements in all areas of his life. He said that he now confided in his wife, had stopped acting as the children's servant, and had become assertive and effective at work—to mention only a few of the improvements. I had to discourage him from producing a paper and pencil in order to write down all the insights gained in sessions. He regretted that he could still report no dreams, but resolved to "try harder next time". When, I began to wonder, would the "nurse leave the child to remain alone with the analyst and start to play"?

For Peter's animation felt as if a most diligent pupil had installed himself with me. Or else, very pleasantly, without patronage, *he* became *my* instructor, concerning his work and other matters in which he was competent, while I was feeling like a supine disciple. It seemed to me at the time as if this alternation of roles between "teacher" and "pupil" militated against Peter's original, express wish to reach his "Real" (True) Self. Having myself been caught up in this stated aim, which chimed with the latent True/False model, I believe that I became inwardly impatient with what I saw largely as a prolonged defensive stance.

After about three months' twice-weekly therapy, Peter arrived late from an important meeting, and devoted an entire session to all the new ways he had found of doing good to others, culminating with the statement, "I really think *this* may be my True Self".

I was aware of feeling intense irritation and frustration at what felt like a monumental exercise in defensive compliance, while managing to remind myself of Peter's claim that I was the first person he had ever talked to about himself. So I simply commented on how all these good things were contrasting with his earlier distress. I tried to persuade myself that perhaps the diligent pupil and teacher guises were necessary and genuine ways of Peter's being present with me, even though they also indicated his desperation to avoid acknowledging, even to himself, the terror of any other kind of exposure. Then, as he was leaving, he asked, almost aggressively, "Are the sessions always fifty minutes?. . . Is there a facility for extra time if I'm late?" To my negative reply, he complained that this seemed "unfair", and, although I said we would discuss it next time, his anger was palpable. But it was left for me to raise the issue again, with Peter restored to his obliging, pedagogic ways.

Forced to review my apparently restrained bearing in the previous session, the unpleasing probability dawned on me that silent disapproval may well have been written all over my face for Peter to read, and then to react to, at the end, by his rare and rather welcome flash of anger. My insistent feeling that Peter was filling his session with False Self strategies and efforts to be a good patient was surely based on the highly questionable fantasy, already mentioned, that there was another, truer part of Peter to be "mine(d)". It is this kind of experience that has led me to suggest that, if transplanted from its original soil, the idea of the True/False Self dichotomy can become the collusion of both patient and analyst. This subverts the therapeutic task of aiding the integration of compliance with other facets of the personality.

This kind of anomaly may have led to a fading of allusions to True/False terminology and to a drift in Winnicott's work towards a more tentative and more multifaceted view of the Self, which is evident not only in his treatment of clinical material, but also in the following introduction to his late extended description:

> [T]here is much uncertainty even in my own mind about [the meaning of "Self"]. . . . For me the self, which is not the ego, is the person who is me, who is only me, who has a totality based on the operation of the maturational process. At the same time the self has parts, and in fact is constituted of these parts. [Winnicott, 1970, p. 271]

This privileges the uniqueness of the original, essential Self, which for Winnicott was never the id, but often seems to have been equated by him with the ego and now is visualized as a "self . . . constituted of parts". This accords in some respects with both post-Jungian and post-Kleinian models of personality and also with Winnicott's concerns, where "aliveness" and "feeling real" feature as the hallmarks of health.

In his definitive exploration of the Self, while still tracing much development to the mother/infant interaction and mirroring, Winnicott, omitting reference to a True/False split, continues:

> The self finds itself naturally placed in the body, but may in certain circumstances become dissociated from the body or the body from it. The self essentially recognizes itself in the eyes and facial expression of the mother and in the mirror which can come to represent the mother's face. [ibid.]

Thus, while retaining the mirroring metaphor and the paradox that "me-ness" depends for its realization on "M/Other-ness", the idea of "dissociation" for the designation of major personality disjunction seems to have arisen especially in relation to patients where the concern is less with a Self split into True and False, than with the question of whether they are, or have, a Self. It avoids both the notion of a clean True/False split and also what we have seen to be the pejorative implication of that antithesis.

When, therefore, we turn finally to Winnicott's later clinical material and reflections on the Self, much of the adult case material relates to the pre-oedipal, schizoid, borderline kind of disorder, where the above concerns are reflected and where there is often a strong sense that the person is only partially present in the room. Such patients may complain of not feeling "here" or not feeling "real", with the well-meant injunction of some analysts—"Just bring yourself"—experienced as a kind of mockery, an impossible challenge. There is less the sense of a False Self conducting the show than of a more multiple splintering, a fissuring of the Self, with a depleted presence, a thinness, a shallowness of being, best expressed by the idea of "dissociation". The internal violence of such a process involves disturbance of the subject's embodiment in both time and space, as vividly depicted by Ferenczi:

> The personality is described as torn in two or more distinct parts and after this disintegration the fragments assume, as it were, the form and function of a whole person. The ego leaves the body, partly or wholly. . . . But the traumatic force catches up and, as it were, shakes the ego down from the high tree or tower like a frightening whirlwind. [Ferenczi, quoted in Chasseguet-Smirgel, 1987, p. 59]

Of one woman patient, Winnicott, referring to her "dissociation", writes: "There is never a whole person there to be aware of the two or more dissociated states that are present at any one time" (1971b, p. 27). Faced with the challenge of how to get into real contact with such a patient, Winnicott watches and waits for ways of easing her out of the dissociated state into beginning to "become a whole person". Another patient, to whom Winnicott assigned a weekly three-hour session, complete with the provision of milk and biscuits, he describes thus: "[After nearly two hours] a clinical change had come about. Now for the first time during this session *the patient seemed to be in the room with me*" (Winnicott, 1971c, p. 60).

And in a further remarkable example, after years of work with a man patient, which had been productive without getting to the heart of the matter, Winnicott suddenly cried, "I am talking to a girl!" (1971a, p. 73). For his openness and sensitivity had led him to this most precise awareness of that dissociated part of the person with whom he was engaging. This realization broke the deadlock and transformed the analysis.

So the emphasis is on the goal of "feeling real" or feeling "alive", of "creativity", the model of a Self composed of diverse parts, which in illness become dissociated and fragmented. With these patients, Winnicott is primarily concerned with the technical and empathic challenge of contacting, engaging with, and integrating sometimes diverse dissociated parts of the personality into the Self. Such an approach is visibly far more flexible and subtle than is implied in the simple True/False dichotomy and avoids regarding the "part" that is present in the room as simply False or a defence to be overcome.

CHAPTER THREE

Winnicott and Lacan: selfhood versus subjecthood

Katherine Cameron

This chapter is an attempt to see what might emerge from a parallel consideration of some of the key concepts of Winnicott and of Lacan as they relate to the topic suggested by my title. Whether or not the juxtaposition of these two purportedly disparate psychoanalysts can be seen as a largely fortuitous one, it might be that each will come to illuminate the other and consequently the entire topic.

The two have very different underlying views of how everything hangs—or does not hang—together. In Lacan's case, he demonstrates his philosophical position—however obscurely—whereas in Winnicott's case, his basic position is largely implicit and in its broad framework could in fact be said to be a set of received assumptions: it is how he takes off—where he goes—from this position that is distinctive.

By looking first at the one area that, on the face of it, suggests an overlap in the ideas of these two psychoanalysts, the nature of any possible similarities and differences might start to become more clear.

Both men, in their consideration of the formation and nature of identity, used the concept of the mirror in more vivid, original, and

pertinent ways than had ever been done before. It is perhaps surpris-
ing to discover that "*La stade du miroir*" [The Mirror Stage], though it
achieved a published form only in 1949, was presented in its original
version in 1936, over thirty years before Winnicott's the "Mirror-Role
of Mother and Family in Child Development" was published in 1967.
This surprise cannot be put down to the "style" of Lacan's piece—as
distinct from its "content". With Lacan such a distinction is meaning-
less. He had assimilated structuralist ways of thinking, and it was
from such an angle that he depicted "the mirror stage".

For the first time, Lacan's infant (between about the age of 6 and
18 months) sees himself alone, separate, rather than in the face of his
mother. The realization brought by this reflection in the mirror is of
something that is not the Self. It is an (ideal) *image* of unity and
autonomy—the ego, which, though it might be inappropriate to call it
a self-delusion, is certainly an illusion, based as it is on an Imaginary[1]
relationship with one's own body. As Lacan says, "This *Gestalt* . . .
symbolizes the mental permanence of the *I*, at the same time as it
prefigures its alienating destination" (1949, p. 2). It is a projection that
divides the human from himself on the basis of this structuring illusion: coherence at the cost of alienation. It seems to the nascent subject
that he is to be found out there, in that image, but there is in fact an
inherent mismatch between this outer and the inner, in that one is not
to be found in the other (the subject and the object are in an obverse
relationship to each other).

Lacan concludes from his account that the structure of the ego and
hence of human knowledge is essentially paranoid in nature. This
derives not merely from the relationship to, and rivalry with, the
image of the individual in the mirror—with the face that is like the
mother's but is not the mother's—but through the identification and
accompanying rivalry with the other like images in the surrounding
space, and with that shared space itself, the world in common. At
this—Imaginary—level of conceptualization there are relationships to
(images of) others, but these relationships are inherently identificatory
and narcissistic in nature and so also productive of aggressivity "as a
correlative tension of the narcissistic structure in the coming-into-

---

[1] Lacan's Imaginary order appertains to the ego, which orientates itself
mainly through identificatory images as evoked during the mirror stage.
Thereafter, it persists, most notably, in close relationships of a narcissistic kind.

being (*devenir*) of the subject" (Lacan, 1948, p. 22). This presents aggressivity as a comparative latecomer on the scene, required to fill a ready-made role and not instrumental in bringing about any major switches of plot. Unlike Winnicott's "aggressive component" it results from, rather than produces, the "coming-into-being".

That this "coming-into-being" of the Lacanian subject brings to mind the "going-on-being" of Winnicott's infant is perhaps fortuitous, because, like the latter, the former seems to maintain itself in this state in perpetuity. That is to say, it is for ever becoming, and never becomes. It expresses a kind of antithesis of take-off to the Winnicottian staying-at-home. It would also be true to add that, at the stage in Lacan with which we are dealing, the individual, mired in the Imaginary, has not yet attained access to the Symbolic. What is being portrayed is a spectral world, a staging post on the way to subjecthood.

The first thing to be said about Winnicott's notion of mirroring is that it is placed earlier in the infant's development than is Lacan's mirror. Nevertheless, at the beginning of his paper on the topic, Winnicott acknowledges that he had been influenced by Lacan's paper, before stating that Lacan had not thought in terms of the mother's face as he himself proposed to do. What is being talked about is identification at a stage before a separating-out from the mother (or environment, in Winnicott's sense) has been completed. What is offered to the baby is recognition of itself in the eyes/face of its mother. This is, of course, different from identifying yourself with another person but is, perhaps, not so different from something described by Lacan in "The Function and Field of Speech and Language in Psychoanalysis" (1953, p. 166): "Man's desire finds its meaning in the desire of the other, not so much because the other holds the key to the object desired, as because the first object of desire is to be recognized by the other." Where the difference between the two certainly does lie is in the outcome. For Winnicott it is to find, and for Lacan to search. What is to be found in Winnicott is your Self (that is, you find it, others perhaps acknowledge it). The latter may be what Winnicott means by his apparently contradictory statements on this matter in "Communicating and Not Communicating Leading to a Study of Certain Opposites" (1963a, pp. 186, 187), and again in "Playing: Creative Activity and the Search for the Self", where on p. 63 Winnicott writes "she exists in the searching rather than in finding or being found", and follows this up on the next page with the following:

> The searching can only come from desultory formless functioning, or perhaps from rudimentary playing, as if in a neutral zone. It is only here, in this unintegrated state of the personality, that that which we describe as creative can appear. This if reflected back, *but only if reflected back*, becomes part of the organized individual personality, and eventually this in summation makes the individual to be, to be found; and eventually enables himself or herself to postulate the existence of the self. [1971c, p. 64]

You are revealed to yourself in the other and given back to yourself, thus achieving Self-awareness. Even though still not totally separated, this confers additionally upon the child a dawning awareness of the wider environment in "the beginning of a significant exchange with the world, a two-way process in which self-enrichment alternates with the discovery of meaning in the world of seen things" (Winnicott, 1967, p. 132). To be seen not only *in* but *by* the Other means to discover both yourself and that there is an other, though the Winnicottian pendulum has a way of always swinging back to the Self, and it sometimes seems as if after the mother there is no other.

Curiously, when later on the "average girl" looks in an actual mirror, "she is reassuring herself that the mother-image is there and that the mother can see her and that the mother is *en rapport* with her" (Winnicott, 1967, p. 132). Whilst this is presumably the internalized mother—an internal object—projected outwards, it is something other than the Self in the mother's face; perhaps an amalgam is assumed: "Where mother is, there I am." The alternative is that the image and the Self have been separated out, producing a kind of parallel to the Lacanian alienation, with the looker in a childlike dependence upon the image for reassurance that she/the Self *does* exist, which is what for Lacan constitutes the mirage. It must be said at once that it is hard to see how this latter interpretation can be made consistent with Winnicott's various references to the central (True) Self as an isolate, and "unaffected by experience" (Winnicott, 1963b, p. 99). It could be revealing to look at and compare two sets of statements, both of which have a relationship to Descartes' *cogito ergo sum*,

Lacan's acknowledged and Winnicott's apparently unconscious. Winnicott introduces his thus:

> I see that I am linking apperception with perception by postulating a historical process (in the individual) which depends on being seen:
> When I look I am seen, so I exist.
> I can now afford to look and see.
> I now look creatively and what I apperceive I also perceive.
> In fact I take care not to see what is not there to be seen (unless I am tired).
>
> [Winnicott, 1967, p. 114]

There are various things to be said about this. The "Other" (as in "seen by an other") is dispensed with. The central concept, "I am seen, so I exist", promotes the passive state as fundamental (bringing to mind Winnicott's contention that "being" has to come before "doing"—see Winnicott, 1945, p. 152). And, finally, it confirms what has been inherent in the notion of "apperception", which is that Selfhood is linked to Self-consciousness. In fact, like Descartes, this model privileges consciousness and presents a startling contrast to Lacan's following formulations: "I think where I am not, therefore, I am where I do not think. . . . I am not wherever I am the plaything of my thought; I think of what I am where I do not think to think" (Lacan, 1957, p. 166).

Winnicott's child has already attained "unit status" before Lacan's has encountered his illusory ego, and, while Winnicott's "ego offers itself for study long before the word Self has relevance", "The word Self arrives after the child has begun to use the intellect to look at what others see or feel or hear and what they conceive of when they meet this infant body" (Winnicott, 1962, p. 56); in other words, following the advent of the awareness described in the "Mirror-Role" paper (1967). Hereafter, there is not always a clear distinction between the Self and ego in Winnicott.

The comparative study of Winnicott and Lacan may now be extended into a consideration of "object-relations".

Lacan's vision is characterized, perhaps above all, by the idea of lack. The loss instituted by the separation of birth can never be made good and so comes to permeate the entire human trajectory. The object can never fill the lack in the subject, because the object itself is lacking. This lack comes to be represented by the phallus as the signifier of an absence, which is nevertheless representable. There is no analogue for this in Winnicott, for whom the mother is a whole rather than a hole. However, it has been suggested (see Roudinesco, 1986, p. 491) that there might be some sort of correspondence between Winnicott's "transitional object" and Lacan's "*l'objet a*", "the object of desire", said to represent what is lacking, but sometimes appearing to be that lack itself, "the nothing" (Lacan, 1960, p. 315), the cut; itself unrepresentable, it cannot be caught in the mirror; an irreducible remnant, it is also referred to as a partial object, not, like the part-object, a part of the total object, but only partially representing "the function that produces [it]" (Lacan, 1960, p. 315).

Certainly, "*l'objet a*" is in no way depicted as having, like the transitional object, the function of bridging the gap between the individual (infant) and the world, in the process of their separating out from each other. Where it stands in for the lack in the form of some object, it is the mother's lack, not the lack of the mother that "*l'objet a*" stands for and can, in fact, through fusion with her actual missing part, be converted into a fetish (as, interestingly, can the transitional object: Winnicott, 1951, p. 236).

The transitional object—the "me–not-me" pre-symbol—does share a quality of apparent ambiguity with the "*l'objet a*":

> It is true that the piece of blanket (or whatever it is) is symbolical of some part-object, such as the breast. Nevertheless, the point of it is not its symbolic value so much as its actuality. Its not being the breast (or the mother) is as important as the fact that it stands for the breast (or mother). [Winnicott, 1951, p. 233]

At any rate, armed with this paradoxical object, the child can begin to tangle with the external world, egged on by his pre-existent "aggressive component", which "drives the individual to a need for a *Not-Me* or an object that is felt to be *external*" (Winnicott, 1950, p. 215) and which, in Winnicott's view of things, does actually have the status of externality, of separateness, and forms part of the process of disillusionment. Unlike object-relating, which "is an experience of the subject that can be described in terms of the subject as an isolate" (Winnicott, 1969, p. 88), the object to be used (in "The Use of an Object") must be "a part of shared reality, and not a bundle of projections" (ibid.). It is attacked and destroyed because it is beyond (om-nipotent) control and is beyond control because of this attack. It survives destruction, and the individual has separated out from its surroundings and can relate to them from this position of relative detachment.

The movement has been from the merged state (with the mother-figure, and surroundings) to that of a separate entity. The use of symbols proper is now possible, but they constitute a set of tools for the realization of what is essentially pre-existent rather than being of themselves an actual condition of the human enterprise (the human subject) as they are for Lacan. For Lacan, entry into the Symbolic[2] field is the potential solution to the problem of imaginary entrapment maintained in the mother–child dyad. The "*nom du père*" comes be-tween the child and its mother, so preventing the child from becoming the mother's missing phallus; this symbolic castration establishes the law of language for the subject, and with it a subjecthood constituted not, as in Winnicott, in a separated-out Self, but in a divided form within the shared field of the signifiers in a state of primary repression.

For in Lacan, apart from the Real[3] (and the Real is apart), objectiv-ity is viewed from the standpoint of subjectivity. Perhaps it could be said that existence resides in the relations between things, not in the things themselves: a theory of relativity, an endlessly moveable feast. It can be seen that this expresses a very different philosophical pos-ition from that occupied by Winnicott, who inhabits a world of discrete entities, however merged they might at times appear to be. It is perhaps ironical—or perhaps not—that it was Lacan who claimed a "return to Freud". You could say that it was a return on his own terms. What most noteworthily reemerged, along with the former pre-eminence of the Oedipus complex, was the concept of desire—minted anew. What slipped from view was the Freudian version of a (real) outside world to be endlessly struggled with. In Winnicott that

---

[2] Lacan's Symbolic order is the dominant and determining order, linked indissolubly to language: the field of the symbolic is the field of signifiers. This is the terrain of the subject.

[3] The Real is that within either the mental or material sphere which, unlike the imaginary, cannot be brought fully into the symbolic process although it is attached to it. It is intractable, unassimilable, like a trauma.

real world—a natural, biological world—is there, but transmuted into an optimally nurturing version as the early supportive environment. Winnicott's infant is biologically constituted, whilst his experiences are preponderantly oriented around a subjective sense of identity. The id is a very poor bedfellow to the ego, the harbinger of the self: "It is indeed possible to gratify an oral drive and by so doing to *violate* the infant's ego-function, or that which will later on be jealously guarded as the Self, the core of the personality" (Winnicott, 1962, p. 57). Nevertheless, this environment—mother and otherwise—starts in the baby's experience by being unseparated from itself, giving rise to the famous dictum, "There is no such thing as a baby", as well as to such coinages as the "environment–individual set-up" (Winnicott, 1952, p. 99), but the environment is an environment for all that and there to be separated out from. It is in this bio-nurturing context that the notion of "need"—though not on this account itself biological—becomes privileged over that of "desire" (see "Primary Maternal Preoccupation", 1956, p. 301). Questions of environment, of course, also raise the issue of adaptation to that environment, a notion of which Lacan was extremely critical. For him the individual is actually constituted by the environment and maintained within it. Through early interaction with, and internalization of, the environment (the *"Umwelt"* of "The Mirror Stage") the individual acquires its very structure and there can be no question of adaptation—or otherwise—to the structuring environment, but only of how to achieve expression from within it. Desire does this. It does it against the background resulting from the aforementioned lack at the heart of existence and is inextricably linked to the notion of the empty subject, to which topic we are finally brought.

The nascent subject is, as we have seen, initially dependent upon the other for recognition and "the subject appears first in the Other" (Lacan, 1973, p. 218). However, this Other, who is at first the mother (M-Other), being a subject too, is also lacking, and so desire is set upon its career, which, with the subsequent advent of the phallic signifier, develops into an endless phantom chase down a chain of signifiers that refer to each other rather than to the underlying subject in a process of perpetual displacements. The subject remains "the place from where"; never visible, never knowable; it is split and de-centred. Winnicott's True Self, on the other hand, though hidden, is potentially accessible to the lone individual, is expressible by a "spontaneous gesture" (Winnicott, 1960, p. 148) and has a place to be, a still quiet place (however under siege it might be), right at the core of the person, tucked away inside, one might say, since this is a world that still retains some well-established contours.

Lacan may play in Winnicott's transitional space, but all the familiar signposts have been removed.

CHAPTER FOUR

The emergence of a sense of Self, or, The development of "I-ness"

Frances Tustin

> "The world of experience belongs to the basic word
> I-It. The basic word I-You establishes the world of relation.
> Relation is reciprocity. . . . We live in currents of universal
> reciprocity."
>
> Martin Buber

I am sure that all of you think of yourself as "I", and can think of me as "You". We tend to take this for granted, and never realize what a remarkable achievement it is. In this chapter, I am going to discuss states that are so early that the sense of self is undeveloped. To do this, I draw from the background of my work as a child psychotherapist, a great deal of which has been with autistic children. In working with these children we can watch the early unfolding of the sense of Self and can begin to realize the miracle of this achievement.

* * *

Clinical work with autistic children has made me aware of a very early phase of personality development in which, metaphorically

speaking, there are the embryonic elements for a Self that is waiting to be born. Intensive psychotherapeutic work with autistic
children makes it clear that in them the unfolding of this budding
Self has not taken place. The potentiality for selfhood is there, but
it has never developed sufficiently for the child to have a sense of
being a Self related to other selves. Autistic children who can
speak show this either by never using the personal pronoun "I", or
by never using it in the proper way to refer to themselves. The
non-speaking autistic children obviously lack a sense of personal
identity. In this chapter, I hope to show that this early arrest of
basic personality development is due to paralysing terrors that, to
those of us whose sense of Self is well established, are likely to
seem bizarre. In working with these children, as these terrors are
relieved, I have seen, in slow motion as it were, the gradual emergence of their sense of being an "I". They do this laboriously,
haltingly, rigidly. In these respects, their belated development in
treatment is very different from that of a normal individual. However, it has seemed to me that, in spite of this, work with such
children can throw light on an early infantile situation, and also on
the difficulties encountered by some neurotic patients whose sense
of personal identity is very insecure.

Let me develop this theme further.

Work with such neurotic patients and with autistic children
has shown me that earliest infancy seems to be a world of sensation experienced in a fluid way. After birth, sensations of being in
the watery medium of the womb appear to linger on. The psycho-
analyst Rene Spitz has pointed out the adjustment that the
newborn infant has to make to change from being a water creature
to being a dweller on dry land. This adjustment takes time. Freud
has drawn our attention to the fact that: "There is much more
continuity between intra-uterine life and earliest infancy than the
impressive caesura of birth allows us to believe" (1926). Clinical
work with elemental states in children confirms this.

Winnicott tells us of how meaningful to him was the line
from Tagore: "On the seashore of endless worlds children play."
In using the term "oceanic feeling" to describe early infantile
states, Freud seems to have had something like this in mind.

The vague poetic intuitions of Tagore and others have been
confirmed by the recent work of certain paediatricians and obste-

tricians. They have found that recordings of sounds from within the womb, such as the mother's heart-beat and the watery noises, have a marked soothing effect on the newborn infant in the early weeks of life. The fact that the infant's early food and excretions are liquid in nature will also reinforce the infant's early sense of fluidity.

The development of autistic children seems to have been halted at this early level. As treatment diminishes their massive withdrawal, they show us the nameless terrors that arise from the sense of fluidity that has permeated their being. They show us that they are afraid of being spilled and of flowing away into nothingness. Certain articulate neurotic patients often convey such early fluid states of "being" in more communicable form than the autistic children can do at the outset of treatment. For these neurotic patients, whose sense of personal identity is very insecure, the early elemental surges, tides, waves, and floods of sensations have not seemed to be encompassed by a "good-enough" "holding situation" nor by the boundary of their own skin. When working at depth with such patients they struggle to tell us about the unspeakable situation that has become hidden away because it was so unbearable.

Here is an example from such a neurotic patient.

The patient, whom I will call Jean, was a 21-year-old woman who, as a 13-year-old girl, had been brought to see me from the local hospital, as such a severe case of Anorexia Nervosa that it was feared she would die. She responded well to intensive psychoanalytic treatment, which was terminated earlier than I had thought advisable when, aged 15, she went to boarding school which was the normal course of events in her family. She returned to me aged 21, of her own volition and paying her own fees, because she had fits of depression. On her return for this second phase of treatment, Jean had been seeing me once a week for one year, when, due to heavy snowfalls, the Christmas holiday was unduly extended.

At first, on her return from this overlong Christmas holiday, Jean chattered somewhat inconsequentially. Finally, she told me about a friend who was drinking heavily. She said that she thought that he did this because he felt so "empty". At this point, she seemed to have settled down to work, so I suggested that during the unduly extended Christmas holiday she had felt empty. I suggested that the chatter had been to cover up how empty she felt she was, just as the friend she had mentioned drank heavily to do this.

After a while, she said that she often felt that we were two jugs pouring into each other. She felt that her jug had a hole in it and that her water spilled out of it. I replied that I thought that her chatter had seemed to be to block up the hole so that she didn't become empty.

There was a long silence after this in which I felt that we were both working over the feeling of being spilled and empty. Jean broke the silence to say that she had been sleeping badly. On the basis of much material from earlier sessions, I suggested that this might be because of the falling sensations in "falling asleep". On the basis of this day's material I said that perhaps she was afraid that she would "fall endlessly" and spill into emptiness. Thoughtfully, Jean agreed and went on to say, somewhat haltingly, as if she were trying to dredge the depths, that "deep down", hidden away, she felt as if she were a "waterfall", "falling and falling out of control" into a "bottomless abyss, into boundless space, into nothingness". She said: "It's the feeling of being out of control as much as the falling which is so frightening. I'm afraid that I shall lose myself."

I responded to Jean by saying that I thought that "deep down" referred to experiences she had had very early in her life. She seemed to be saying that in the beginning of her life she had felt that she was composed of fluids which could be spilled so that she lost all sense of being a self—of existing. She said "Yes! Yes!", as if this was very meaningful to her. I went on to remind her that in the early days of her analysis, when she first came to me suffering from Anorexia, she had told me that she had felt relieved when her periods stopped because she had always been afraid that she would bleed to death. I said that being afraid that she would lose her existence was even worse than being afraid that she would die from bleeding to death. If she died, at least she would leave her body behind, but if she stopped existing, it would be complete annihilation, nothing would be left. She would be a "no-body"—a "non-entity". This seemed very meaningful to her, for she had often talked to me about her feeling that she was a non-entity.

After a short pause, she reminded me of a remark she had made in the first phase of her analysis about something that we had both recognized to be an illusion. She had said: "I know it's an illusion, but the terror is real." I replied that I thought this applied to the terror of losing her existence—of becoming a "no-body". She knew that it was an illusion, but the terror was real. There was silence whilst I felt that we both experienced this terror. I broke the silence to ask her what she was thinking. She said that she was thinking of the hymn,

> Time like an ever-rolling stream
> Bears all its sons away
> They fly forgotten as a dream
> Dies at the opening day.

This girl came from a religious background, so I said that in states of terror to think about a hymn was often comforting. I went on to say that in this session I had noticed that we had both kept referring to the previous phase of her analysis before she went to boarding school. Perhaps the unduly long Christmas holiday had re-evoked the feelings she had had between the ending of that first phase and her return to analysis for this second phase. She had told me that during the time when she was at boarding school, and afterwards she had been afraid that I would forget her and that she would forget me. She was showing me that, hidden in the depths of her being, "forgetting" was the feeling of everything being spilled out of her and out of me. She experienced this as losing her sense of existence of feeling "gone".

Some time ago, I presented Jean's material in the Watford Child Guidance Clinic, after which one of the workers there called Michael Whan sent me a paper he had written called "Lethe, Time and Forgetting". He had been struck by Jean's use of the image of herself as a jug with a hole in it, and with my linking it to the fear of being spilled and equating this with an early experience of "forgetting". Michael Whan's paper was based on the Greek myth in which Lethe is the Spring of Forgetfulness, which is found in the Underworld. In the paper, he tells us that connected with Lethe "was a condition of the soul which was likened to that of a leaky pitcher". He goes on to say that leaking was associated with forgetting. He also says: "Lethe, in its temporal meaning places the notion of 'being hidden' in terms of time's concealing course; the way that events and happenings in time become concealed in time's distancing flux and remote depths." This echoes the common phrase, "the mists of time". It also echoes the hymn quoted by Jean.

Obviously, at these levels, we are dealing with forms of experience from which the myths have sprung. We also seem to be dealing with the poetic levels of personality. The poet Louis MacNeice was in touch with these early fluid states of "being" and the paradoxical terrors arising from them. In the last verse of his poem "Prayer Before Birth", he poignantly describes them. Giving the verse the form and shape of a waterfall, he writes:

> I am not yet born; O fill me
> with strength against those who would freeze my
> humanity, would dragoon me into a lethal automaton,
> would make me a cog in a machine, a thing with
> one face, a thing, and against all those
> who would dissipate my entirety, would
> blow me like thistledown hither and
> thither or thither and hither
> like water held in the
> hands would spill me.
> Let them not make me a stone and let them not spill me.
> Otherwise kill me.

MacNiece expresses very well the dramatic extremes by which autistic children feel so threatened. There is the uncontrollable fluidity, but there is also the intransigent immobility of a stone.

MacNiece also realized that to live permanently in a world of such acute extremes is lethal: such extremes cannot be borne—

they have to be consigned to oblivion. In working with these children, we are also prone to sink "lethewards" and to become as lethargic as they are. An important part of our work is to struggle against this.

After many years of working with them, I have come to realize that their lethargy is a reaction to avoid the hypersensitized extremes of sensation in which they would otherwise live. Such hypersensitivity seems to be a perpetuation and intensification of an early infantile state.

Let me develop this theme further.

Winnicott alerted us to the hypersensitized responses of the mother to her newborn infant. He pointed out that such responses would be abnormal at any other time. It has seemed to me that the newborn infant is also unusually sensitive. Such mutual ultra-sensitivity would facilitate the establishment of primal bonds between mother and baby. As both mother and baby enjoy the ordinary effortful realities of the suckling, toileting, and grooming activities of early infancy, the extraordinary hypersensitivity begins to wane. Metaphorically speaking, as the fluid states of earliest infancy begin to subside, both the mother and child "come down to earth". The child becomes "rooted" in the "earth mother", who, with the support of the father, introduces the child to the more ordinary world of common sense with its inevitable limitations, but which also brings reassurances. Infants who are autistic from at, or near, birth are invariably reported as being difficult to suckle. Also, they rarely, if ever, suck their fingers or their thumbs. I suspect that this deficiency in sucking has a deleterious effect upon the development of their mental patterns and is one factor in their seeming mental defect. Such children are often described as "backward". In my view this is because they have remained in, or have retreated to, an early state of fluid sensuousness.

In normal development, this early fluid sensuousness soon becomes channelled through sucking, wriggling, kicking, and other ideomotor activities. It is also expressed through the little dramatic plays that develop between mother and baby, as also through such things as lullabies, nursery rhymes, fantasies, singing games, and fairy stories. Later, it finds expression in play, in games, in myths, in poetry, in drama—in short, in all the symbolic aesthetic and cognitive activities the human being is privileged to be heir to. The autistic individual has missed all this. For a variety of reasons, excesses of sensuous tension experienced as accumulations of fluids have interrupted and prevented the development of an on-going reciprocal relationship with the parents who, in my experience, have usually been ready and waiting to respond. Alone and unaided, the autistic child has struggled to deal with the overwhelming turgidity of these tensions. His primal hypersensitivity remains unmodified and unexpressed through symbolic activities with other people. Due to this avoidance of reciprocal channels of expression, the unmodified floods of excitation become intensified beyond all bearing and cause trouble. As one patient explained to me about states of ecstatic pleasure, "They are too rich. I can't digest them." Like other such patients she had protected herself by shutting out the sources of such pleasure, people being the most exciting source. Cutting off the focus of attention is one of the earliest forms of protection. The autistic child uses this elemental mode of protection in a massive way. It results in a hypersensitized child appearing insensitive, impenetrable, and lacking in empathy.

Recently, I read an interesting paper by the father of an autistic girl called Ellie. Some of you may know the book written by Ellie's mother. In it, she describes how all the family helped Ellie to emerge from her autism to some degree. The mother was Mrs Raiburn Park and the book is called *The Siege*, because Mrs Park felt that they laid "siege" to the "empty fortress" of Ellie's autism. The father's paper was published in the *Journal of Autism and Childhood Schizophrenia*. It was brought to my notice by Mrs Elizabeth Irvine because she felt it confirmed what I had said in my recent book *Autistic States in Children* (1981) about the autistic child's difficulties in tolerating extreme states of ecstatic sensuous pleasure. The father describes how Ellie could not stand states of what he called "rapture". Such states would come, for example, when she saw the beauty of the moon behind a pine tree. When she was 12 years old, Ellie drew pictures to show what she did when extreme states of sensuousness were too much for her. She showed that sometimes she needed two doors, sometimes three doors, and sometimes four doors to shut out the impact of such upsetting states.

It is significant that we use the word "upset" to describe the reaction to unbearable states. It has in it the notion of fluids being spilled. This word always reminds me of an amusing incident that occurred many years ago in the Tavistock Clinic when Dr John Bowlby was the medical director of the Department of Children and Parents. A guest from abroad, whose English was a little shaky, wanted to compliment Dr Bowlby on the "set-up" of the Clinic, but he said "Dr Bowlby what a fine upset you have here." Well, autistic children have an "upset" rather than a "set-up". In this chapter I want to show you how some of them become "set-up" as a person in their own right with an upright sense of being an "I", instead of feeling "upset" and spilled away.

At these elemental levels, states of extremity are experienced as their "cup being full and running over". It is important that the therapist should not be a "crackpot"—that is, that he or she should be sane and sensible. The child needs to feel that there is a "non-cracked pot", or an intact jug, or a non-leaky pitcher that can hold the overflows of impulsive sensuous tension until he can begin to express them through the wonderful symbolic activities which become such an important part of the human being's repertoire. Ellie, like other autistic children, had courageously tried to manage them by an omnipotent magic exclusive and peculiar to herself. This had prevented her from using the help of her parents.

It seems to me that those of us who work with autistic children would do well to listen to William Blake, who wrote that "Men are admitted into Heaven, not because they have curbed and governed their passions"—that is, like Ellie they have built doors— "[and so] have no passions, but because they have cultivated their understanding".

The dictionary tells me that the word "understanding" comes from the Anglo-Saxon word "understandum" which means to "stand under or amid a thing". To help these children we need "to stand under or amid" the extremes of their elemental states of "being" and to find resonances within ourselves. In short, we need to be able to empathize with them. Such children's own lack of empathy makes this a difficult task.

As the therapist "feels with" the child and holds him in the professional and disciplined understanding that encourages sensible behaviour, a structure emerges in the child. He becomes less at the mercy of formless, unbounded impulsive fluid sensations. They begin to feel channelled. Their flow begins to feel directed and held. He begins to respond to the therapist, who, as Marion Milner has so well said, "is the servant of a process". As the child begins to allow the therapist to help him to bear and to channel extreme states of fluid sensation instead of feeling so overwhelmed by them that he "passes out" into oblivion, both child and therapist pass through intense states of terror, anguish, rage, and ecstasy. It is a veritable Garden of Gethsemane. As their intensity becomes more bearable by being shared with someone else, the child begins to be able to tolerate the separateness and the uncontrollability of the "not-me", "not-known", exciting "You" people around him. He begins to respond to and to cooperate with them. He begins to be able to feel that he is an "I", and to use the pronoun "I" to refer to himself. For all of us, the achievement of individuality is a difficult and painful task; for the autistic child, it is much more so.

In order to demonstrate this process in action, I will now take you through an autistic child's psychotherapy up to the time when his personal identity was becoming well established. This synopsis of part of an autistic child's psychotherapy will demonstrate the transformation of the unbounded, boundless flowing-away fluid states, into the sense of having a solid, bounded, coherent, and intact body image which persists in time and space. This was extremely significant to his sense of being an "I".

> The child, whom we will call Antonio, was in treatment with an Italian psychotherapist, Dr Suzanne Maiello. I had the privilege of supervising the early part of this child's treatment. Antonio was referred to Dr Maiello when he was 5½ years old. He was seen three times a week. He was a severe case of Kanner-type autism. Maiello recorded her first impression of him as follows:
>
>> "His large green eyes seemed not to see, and to slip away from me and other objects. He did not speak but produced inarticulate sounds every now and then, and did not usually react to my interpretations."

In the fluid states I talked about earlier, Antonio seemed to float rather than to walk. This impression partly came from the fact that he walked on his toes, with very light, floating movements. It also came from the fact that, during this early period, he climbed to quite high up, using the wooden frames of the door and window as he did so. He did this effortlessly as if supported by water or air. This climbing occurred when he found Maiello's presence too stimulating. These children find it difficult to cope with the intense surges of excitement aroused by contact with people. Unable to use Maiello's ability to hold him safely through these excitements, he fled away from her.

The poet James Greene knew about this dilemma of too much sensuous tension, and he knew the answer. In a poem called "Flash-Back" in his book *Dead Man's Fall* (1980), he wrote:

If I cannot suck
My thumbs
If like lightning I all-but crack—
A minus, non-plussed—
Will you hold me—criss-cross—in your arms,
A gentle straitjacket? . . .
Oh fuse me with the surplus of the thunder
Whose brain is racked
And under fire. . . .

After a time, Antonio turned to Maiello for help with these racking excitements. This change was heralded by his becoming afraid of birds flying. He still did not speak, but in various ways he showed Maiello that he wanted her to put them in a cage so that they would not fly higher and higher and be "gone". He also showed that he was afraid that *he* might be "gone".

Maiello did not put Antonio into a cage but, metaphorically speaking, she held him "criss-cross in her arms", through his extreme states of pleasure or terror, or anguish or rage. She did this by her vigilant awareness and empathic understanding. She also gave him a firm and consistent treatment setting. She did not allow him to wander from room to room. In the consulting room Antonio had a certain amount of freedom, but there were also inevitable and necessary frustrations. For example, there were locked doors to rooms that he was not allowed to enter. When he became aware of these frustrations, as well as angering him they also stimulated his curiosity and his imagination. Sometimes Antonio fantasied that there were wonderful Maiello things in the closed rooms, and sometimes that there were threatening things. These were important developments. For one thing, autistic children do not have fantasies. To develop these was a progress. Also, Antonio was now becoming interested in, and curious about, the therapist and about the outside world. His attention was becoming focused. Also, the capacity to have imaginations about *unseen* things was an important step. Antonio began to live less in a world of bodily sensations and the terrors associated with these. Instead he began to have pictures in his mind. These pictures could embody some of his sensuous excitements.

Antonio's next step was to develop the realistic notion that his body had continuity of existence and could not flow away or dissolve into nothingness. This was shown by his play with tunnels, which indicated that he was being born as a psychological being who existed in time and space.

On one occasion Antonio used the carpet to make a tunnel. He crawled through this tunnel several times "with great involvement and concentration", as Maiello said. When he came out of the carpet tunnel into the light after the long crawling in the dark, there was "an expression of deep surprise on his face". Later in treatment he did the same thing with a small toy sheep, which he made to go through a paper tunnel. As it emerged, he greeted it with an exclamation of "Here it is!", in a tone both of "relief and confirmation of an expected event". Antonio was obviously gaining reassurance that both he and the toy sheep could still exist even though they were out of sight and were not being looked at. His Berkleyan notions were being modified. He was realizing that things, of which his body was one, had continuity of existence apart from being seen, touched, and handled as physical objects. These developments took place partly as the result of reality-testing, but also by Antonio feeling that *he* had omnipotent control over the comings and goings of things—he tried to feel that he was so powerful that in a god-like way he could make things "here", and he could make things "gone".

However, a few sessions later, play developed in which he showed that he was beginning to be able to bear the fact that things could be *out of his magical control*, but could still exist. This concerned his interest in some water pipes. This material illustrates very well the tiny details of perceptual and cognitive development that were occurring in Antonio. Antonio became very interested in the water flowing out of the outlet hole in the wash basin down the outlet pipe and under a grating in the floor. He also put his ear to the pipe that channelled the rush of water when the toilet was flushed. The existence of the water in these pipes could be *inferred*, but it could neither be seen nor directly controlled by him.

There were also indications concerning the nature of his body image during this period. As he was washing his foot, Antonio asked, "What is inside my foot?", as if he thought that it, too, might have pipes. The image of the body as a tube or as a system of pipes is a common one in psychotic children and in regressed adult patients. With Antonio, the equivalence of his body with a similar situation outside probably helped to diminish the sharpness of his awareness of his bodily separateness from the outside world. To some extent, he and it were identical.

Later, however, Antonio began to be able to bear the fact that he was separate and different from things outside his body. He began to realize that his body had a definite boundary and had cohesion and distinctive form and shape. More important still, he began to realize that things had names and that he had a name that distinguished him from others. This was shown in the following way.

When he was 8-years-old, in a fit of temper due to some frustration Antonio pulled a toy lion to pieces. He had brought this lion from home. It was made of plastic sticks assembled in such a way that it could be stretched and shortened like an accordion. After he had dismantled it, Antonio tried to put it together again. But he did it in such a haphazard way that it became a very jumbled-up object. In the next session, Antonio took the ill-assembled lion and, taking it to pieces, he put the pieces into Dr Maiello's lap. Since he was obviously asking for help, Maiello proceeded to put the lion together again in the proper way so that it looked like a lion. When it was finished, Antonio examined the put-together lion and then fetched another toy lion, which was part of the play material provided by Dr Maiello. This toy lion could not be taken to pieces. He compared this cohesive, intact lion with the put-together concertina lion and then said the name "lion". In the following session, Antonio took the key of the drawer in which his toys were kept, and, detaching the label that was hanging from the key, he wrote his own surname and Christian name on it, saying his name as he did so. Antonio was realizing that just as the gathered-together lion could have a name, so when he was gathered together as a separate person he also could have a name. As you will realize, this was a very important step. He was beginning to have a clear sense of his separate and different identity.

Following the lion material, the parents brought further information concerning Antonio's progress. This concerned Antonio's interest in the *objective* appearance of his body as distinct from his subjective experience of it as a system of pipes equated with those in the outside world. The parents reported that Antonio would play for hours looking at his image in a long mirror and then obliterating it with soapy water. He would then wipe the soap off the mirror so that his image reappeared again. Since the parents reported that, during this period of mirror-play, Antonio had recognized a photograph of himself, he must have realized that the mirror-image was of *his* body.

This play in front of the mirror and his play with the carpet tunnel, and with the toy sheep that went through a tunnel and was "there" and was "gone", is reminiscent of the play of the 18-month-old normal baby described by Freud in *Beyond the Pleasure Principle* (1920). It will be remembered that this baby threw a cotton-reel, tied on to his cot by a string, over the side of the cot, saying "gone" when it disappeared, and "there" when he triumphantly pulled it up again. Also, the same normal baby is reported by Freud as looking at his image in the mirror and saying "there", and then, when he bent down below the level of the mirror and the image disappeared, saying "gone". (The relation of this play, to the "Beep-bo" games played by mothers and babies will be obvious.) Freud's normal baby was 18-months-old when he went through these play realizations. Antonio had to wait until he was 8 or 9 years old before he achieved them.

However, belated though it was, in recognizing the mirror-image and the photograph as representations of himself, Antonio was moving towards the notion of "self-representation". Related to this, important new developments took place in his sessions with Maiello. Antonio showed that he was realizing that if he were to make a representation of an object, the image he had in his mind had to have some consonance with the actual external appearance of the object, even though his representation was in a different medium. It could then be used as a symbolic substitute for the object in order to call it to mind. He was becoming less dependent on the presence of the physical object. He was becoming a psychological being. In a beautifully detailed piece of observation, Maiello records this important step of progress as follows:

"Suddenly with great determination, Antonio fetches a sheet of paper and the scissors, and begins to cut the paper. I feel that he is cutting out something, the image of which he has in his mind. He cuts a strip of paper and then cuts it into four squares. He is sitting on the floor with his legs wide apart and put the squares in a line in front of himself between his legs. Then he looks at the chest of drawers which holds his and the other children's toys, and copies the arrangement of the drawers, two on top and two underneath. He repeatedly looks at the original until his reproduction is perfect.

"Then he starts cutting more squares, always four from a strip. If there happens to be five of them, he throws away the fifth one. On his left-hand side, he makes other copies of the chest of drawers, with the paper squares. When doing the first two copies, he looks at the prototype between his legs to check that it is correct, but he never returns to looking at the actual chest of drawers to check the correctness of his representation. Finally, the other copies are done without looking at the actual chest of drawers or at the prototype between his legs. He does these last ones from memory".

It was around this time that Antonio began to use the pronouns "I" and "You" quite correctly and with unfailing accuracy. He was realizing that, through the psychological processes of memory, recollection, and representation, objects (of which he is one) could be felt to have continuity of existence, even though they might not be present to be seen, touched, and handled. That is, they had a psychological dimension. He was also beginning to be able to bear enjoyment. Thus, things that had been seen and enjoyed could, in Wordsworth's words, "flash upon that inward eye which is the bliss of solitude". The aloneness of being an "I" could begin to be tolerated. Individuality was beginning to be established. Later, as the glaze of complacency begins to crack and bland assumptions are given up, self-acceptance becomes a possibility. But this is another story.

This story has concerned the development and establishment of the sense of being an "I". It has been told in evocative and empathic language rather than in theoretical terms. Our language, which has been evolved for the description of objects, is not well adapted to the discussion of non-verbal psychological states. Metaphors help us to do this.

Through these means, I have tried to show that a basic condition for the development of a sense of Self is the feeling that impulses experienced as overwhelming floods of sensation can, through another person's empathic understanding, seem to be received, contained, recycled, regulated, and appropriately directed in a way that ensures that spontaneity is not damaged. Thus, the "waterfalls", the "volcanoes", and such-like uncontrollable overflows do not interrupt the processes of "flowing-over-at-one-ness" which take place between caretaker and naive child, for he is held "criss-cross" in the arms of this caring person's empathic awareness.

In Winnicott's terms, the "holding situation" that is the necessary precondition for a secure and authentic foundation for being an "I" becomes established. The child becomes "rooted" in an "earth-mother". Basic trust becomes established. Metaphorically speaking, the child comes to feel that he has an intact Noah's Ark against the threat of floods and tempests. Within this protection, "one-ness" can become "two-ness". Pairing and sharing begins to be tolerated. He can become an "I" in relation to the "Thou".

* * *

As a summary to this chapter, let me quote from Tennyson's "In Memoriam":

> The baby new to earth and sky,
>   What time his tender palm is prest
>   Against the circle of the breast
> Has never thought that this is I;
>
> But as he grows he gathers much
>   And learns the use of "I" and "me",
>   And finds "I am not what I see,
> And other than the things I touch."
>
> So rounds he to a separate mind
>   From whence pure memory may begin
>   As through the frame that binds him in
> His isolation grows defined.

CHAPTER FIVE

Looking after the Self

Ken Wright

"These fragments I have shored against my ruins."

T. S. Eliot, *The Waste Land*

Winnicott's 1967 paper on the mother's face as the child's first mirror was a major breakthrough in this area of theorizing. But I try to show in this chapter how some of the findings of empirical infant research can greatly extend and enrich the way we think about the development of subjectivity. Stern's work (1985), and in particular what he says about attunement, seems to me to be especially important. It gives us a way of thinking about the relation between the Self and those forms (which come from the Other) *through* which, and *in spite of which*, it attempts to realize itself. It highlights the fact that the Self is essentially dialogic—it exists *only* within a never-ending *dialogue* with the Other which is heir to the earliest dialogue of mother and baby.

As a child I used to dread Sundays. We had to go to church morning and evening and we were not allowed to play. But worse than this were the long, long sermons. Introducing what he said with a biblical text, the preacher would tease out its "Truth" through endless variations. Only when boredom, guilt, and fear had all but destroyed us would he reach an end, there being no further direction he could possibly take.

I now realize that the point of such sermons was to frighten us into believing. But the experience was one of suffocation, and the problem was how to survive. Outwardly, we had to conform and questions were not allowed; inwardly, the important thing was to keep resisting and repudiating—the very life of the Self demanded that this be so.

Years later I did my psychoanalytic training and could not help feeling that I had been here before. Maybe it was all transference (or maybe not), but often in seminars I thought I could recognize the ingredients of my childhood Sundays: the "text" which came from Freud, or one of his "disciples"; the application to every nook and cranny of clinical life; and, worst of all, the requirement of enthusiastic belief. It is true that lip-service was given in these seminars to free discussion of ideas, but in reality this could be only *within* the limits of the text. To question a basic assumption was definitely heretical; and to risk this, as occasionally I did, prompted fears of excommunication, of being chucked out of the training. As in childhood, the easiest and least dangerous option was to sit things out. After all, when I had qualified I would not have to believe if I did not want to.

It is true these preachers made an impression on me, but mainly as examples to be avoided. I prefer to emulate the great essayists such as Montaigne and Emerson, whose writings I discovered as I sought to escape these early constraints. And what lessons they gave with their free interplay of ideas! "Commandeer your freedom", they seemed to say. "Follow your thoughts wherever they go—and do not be afraid! This way you'll discover the truths that *really* matter." For me, their free thinking was a wonderful antidote to the closed minds of the preachers. And so it was that, long before I stumbled on Freud, I discovered the liberating power of free association.

But *institutionalized* Freud is a different matter—as I later found— with its texts and readings from the twenty-four volumes, its concordances and glossaries of terms. So here in this chapter no texts, no revealed or established truths! Nothing indeed to believe in! Only an evocative title—like a first squiggle to respond to.

Respond to! In this idea of responding lies, I think, an essential part of the spirit of psychoanalysis that Winnicott rediscovered in the playfulness of the Squiggle game. In this game, and in his work generally, it is surely the interactive, responsive dimension that is so apparent and important. Not just one *idea* responding to another (free association), but one *person* responding to another (what we might call the free interplay of persons): "Here is a piece of me! How will you respond to that?" It was this responding, or failure in responding, that Winnicott was concerned with in practically all he wrote. In his formulation of *the True and False Self*, for example, it is the Other's *response* that is critical for the Self's fate.

The importance of the Other's response for the Self is also central to what I want to say here. If we see Winnicott as emphasizing *the spontaneous gesture* of the infant, I would want to add that this gesture, at the same time, is an interaction. The spontaneous gesture—the Self's utterance—is in these terms a kind of question from the Self to the Other; it searches for, and hopes to find, a confirming answer.

My purpose, then, is not to write a treatise on the Self—I think the Self does not like to be tied down in too much theory. Instead, I want to clarify certain aspects of self-experience that have a bearing on the integrity and "reality" of the Self. To do this I shall draw on my own experience; and, in doing so, I hope to illuminate Winnicott's ideas about the True and False Self (see chapter one).

Let me go back to my original mentors who believed that they possessed "the Truth"—the one and only Truth that the Self needed. This Truth belonged to them, and they had to enlist everyone else to their point of view. They taught certainties. For them there was only one way of seeing things—their own—and to question this, or to try to see things for oneself, was to err from the truth and be a child of the Devil. The view of these preachers was thus totalitarian and demanded conformity; to accept it meant, in Winnicott's terms, the death of the True Self.

In this scenario, then, the True Self is *in opposition* to the Truth. Two different views of the truth are implied, two different ideas as to what the Self "needs". The first view says that the salvation lies in accepting *the Truth of the Other*; the second that it lies in searching and finding and being guided by one's own soul. We could call this second truth *the Truth of the Self*. You can see that I am tracking

Winnicott quite closely here, making a link between holding to *the Truth of the Self* and being a *True Self* and submitting to the *Truth of the Other* and being a *False Self*. In this scenario, the Truth of the Other is always more or less imposed and endangers creativity. The Other is in-doctrinator (shoving something in), not educator or facilitator (drawing something out).

I believe that the True Self will always in some degree fight for its life in these circumstances, and this was certainly my own experience—something in me would not allow this indoctrination to happen. However conforming I was outwardly, I knew that I *must* preserve my inner integrity. There is a kind of absolute of the Self here—to safeguard one's own truth (the Truth of the Self), one *has* to look after one's Self and protect it from the Truth of the Other.

All this may sound rather paranoid, but it depends on where you find yourself whether paranoia is justified or not. There really are people out there who (at least unwittingly) can harm the Self, and this is one of the things with which Winnicott was concerned. Louis MacNeice was also concerned with such experience, and he graphically evokes this in his poem "Prayer Before Birth".

> I am not yet born; Oh hear me,
> Let not the bloodsucking bat or the rat or the stoat or the
>   club-footed ghoul come near me.
>
> [MacNeice, 1964]

Or, "the human race . . . with tall walls wall me . . . old men lecture me, bureaucrats hector me, mountains/frown at me . . ." and so on. I read MacNeice's poem as an invocation to "someone" who might look after the unborn (not yet realized?) True Self and protect it from this death by Truth (indoctrination) that I am talking about.

Looking after the Self is thus a matter of great importance, and I now want to consider, with some reference to my own experience, what it might involve. While, in favourable circumstances, the Self gets looked after by those around it, this does not happen all the time, and for some people it happens very little. So I want to give some thought to what the Self might do in such circumstances—what ways the Self might find to mitigate the damage of "not good-enough Othering" and how the Self might use the environment in order to *create for itself* an Other that is more helpful and facilitating.

One thing is clear: the Self must learn how to "suss out" what people are "about": who is "good" for the Self and who is "bad" for it; who will look after it and who will threaten it. It is as though whatever else a person does, he must search people and things for their value to the Self—their "soul value". The self-psychologists might talk here about *self-objects*; Winnicott would refer to the adaptive mother or facilitating environment. But more important than the term used is the idea that in order to look after ourselves we have to develop "sensors", or "feelers", with which to explore the environment: "This person is dangerous. . . . Here I smell dogma", for example; "But wait a minute, this situation is different. Here I can breathe, expand, and feel myself coming to life." If the Self is to flourish, true helpers have to be distinguished from false ones.

The implication here is that the Self knows what it needs but has to search it out in the real world and maybe even create it if it cannot be found.

Let me give an example from the realm of theory and theory-making. What is a good theory? A good theory is one that fits the facts. But if we are dealing with psychological theories—theories about the Self—a good theory is one that fits the *subjective* "facts"—in other words, that fits the Self. The important point here is that something from outside (a concept) has to fit with something from inside (an element of subjective experience or a subjective "fact") and we learn to sense very immediately whether such "fitting" is there or not. To think of psychological theory in this way is to link it very closely with issues of the Self, and it starts to become clear *why* people often invest in their theories so emotionally and fight about them so vigorously. It is not so much the "objective theory" (the conceptual structure) that is being contended; rather, it is the case that each person puts a part of his own Self into the theory he has espoused and then feels it to be a container of his own subjectivity (his own Self). In the terms I used earlier, it is the Truth of the Self that is in question and being fought over, not the validity of the theory in any more objective sense. When the *theory* is challenged, it is the *Self* that feels threatened: "Go away and stop interfering with me! I don't want your Truth imposed on my Self!"

This risk—that one's own perception of the Truth (the Truth of the Self) will in some way be obscured by existing concepts (the Truth of the Other)—influences my own attempts to make sense of my experience (in other words, to make theory). When I write, I tend to avoid conventional theory, though obviously I still have preferences. So it might be asked: "If your preference is for Winnicott, as evidently it is, would it not be simpler just to 'talk Winnicott' rather than making your own theory?" Well, it certainly would be simpler, but the danger is that in "talking Winnicott" I will find Winnicott's truth and miss my own. Or someone else will "talk Winnicott" as though Winnicott possessed the Truth and, in turn, attempt to impose this on to my experience. In this way, something initially facilitating and helpful (Winnicott's ideas) can become stultifying; that which had looked after the Self can begin to destroy it. For this reason, I prefer, like Merleau-Ponty (1962), to go "back to the phenomena . . . and take nothing for granted that men, learned or otherwise, believe they know". This radical message of phenomenology is a message the True Self likes to hear; and I am sure it is in this vein that Nina Farhi (1993, p. 104), quoting Masud Khan, writes of each person needing to create, or recreate, their own Winnicott. In some sense, recreating or finding my own Winnicott is what I am doing in this chapter. But I am not writing it *in order* to do this; I am writing to discover for myself what I think (my own truth), and I make use of Winnicott insofar as his ideas help me. For the True Self, ideas are servants; only for the False Self are they gods.

In writing, then, I create my own fragment of theory, and I do this in order to make clear to myself some aspects of my own experience. Capturing an insight in this way—realizing *an aspect of one's own Self* within a symbolic form—is part of what I mean by holding to the Truth of the Self. In these terms, my fragment of Self-created theory is a fragment of my "truth", Winnicott's theories are an aspect of his, and so on. According to this view, each theory-maker develops his own theory, not only in order to define the world, but to provide a support and dwelling-place for elements of his own being.

All this may sound solipsistic and narcissistic, but it does also have a more interpersonal dimension. When I make a bit of theory out of experience, I feel good about it—it is my personal discovery. But this soon moves to a more interpersonal phase—I want you to be interested in my discovery as well. I show it to you and want you to share in it: "What do you make of this? Do you resonate to it? Find an echo of your own experience (Self) in it?" If you say "Yes!", this will somehow enhance my experience. I will feel linkage with you, knowing that my Self has made contact with your Self through the medium of creation. But such a connection is not essential to this process I am describing. My search for something that fits my experience and embodies it for me remains primarily something that I do for myself. It is a self-enclosed experience and is indeed part of what I mean by "looking after the Self".

* * *

In the next part I want to play around with the idea that looking after the Self involves "sensing" or "feeling out" qualities of the object and perhaps discovering or creating them if what is needed is not available. I have touched on this earlier, but now I want to see if I can take it further.

I am supposing that each person "knows", though probably not cognitively, what is essential for his well-being and knows too when he has found it. Let us suppose, then, that each person goes about his business in "searching mode". Whatever else he is doing, his sensors are tuned to the environment and bring back information of relevance to the Self from out there. If the person gets near to something that is needed, his sensors start vibrating—they alert him to investigate more closely. My model reminds me of the childhood game of looking for hidden objects. Someone says, "You're getting warm!", and so you look harder. Or they say, "You're not very warm", and you try turning your attention in other directions. In the game, the prompt comes from another person, but, in the situation I am imagining, the prompt comes from within the person—from his own sensors.

Here is a more concrete example from my own experience: as a child, I spent a lot of the time wandering about on my own. In some ways, the world was not as dangerous as now, and my mother gave me considerable freedom to wander as I pleased. So, for me, the fields, the woods, the trees, perhaps even the sky were like an extension of home. They were part of my territory—a kind of outreach of it—but one in which I could feel alive and nourished, rather than oppressed and hemmed in.

In this mode, then, I felt like lord of my own kingdom. Although I was alone, I found "soul-food" everywhere—the shapes and sounds, the colours and smells of the natural world were all there to support me. *I was alone, but when I reached out, something responded.* You can imagine how readily I warmed to the poet Wordsworth when I discovered him years later! He was talking of *my* experience when he wrote of nature as a *presence* by which one feels in some way looked after.

Nature, of course, is not always experienced in this way; nor would I suggest that there is in fact a spirit in nature which some can sense and others cannot. I am merely saying that the natural world can lend *itself* to being experienced in this way when a person reaches out towards it from a particular state of need. The Self searches . . . and finds where it can. I am talking, of course, of the *True Self* and the indirect and derivative ways by which a person looks after it.

Perhaps, thus far, my central thought is this: *that some process exists by which we can reach out from ourselves towards what is outside ourselves, and that if we are lucky, or if we are blessed, this may lead us to find a form answering to our own subjectivity.* It is the idea of something "out there" resonating or responding to a something "in here" which is the key issue, and I think one can see that this is different from something being merely *projected* into the object. Part of the difference lies in the sensed "fit" or equivalence between two things; another part, in the sense of relatedness and *quasi*-interaction between them. The thing that is "out there" seems, in fact, to *respond* to the thing that is "in here"—it does not merely act as a receptacle for it.

* * *

I am now going to try to link what I have said more explicitly with Winnicott's theory of the True and False Self. Like Winnicott, I am assuming that we have within us, from very early in life, a central Self. Through its "sensors" or "feelers" this Self searches the environment more or less continuously for vital supplies, for that which resonates with it. Just as the organism searches for food, so the Self searches for this other kind of vital nourishment. This nourishment, or "self-food", is always *objective*, in the sense of being "out there", and when found it creates an experience of self-enhancement. In such moments it could be said that the Self has found something that *corresponds* to its need; or that the Self has found an Other who answers to its call. It could also be said that the Self has experienced a *resonance* of itself in the Other, or has felt *recognized* in some important way by the Other. All these ways of talking capture something about the experience that at one time or another would feel true. All are ways of describing an *interaction* with the outside world which enhances the developing sense of Self.

This way of talking links closely with what Winnicott says about the infant's earliest relationship with the breast and later creation/discovery of the transitional object (Winnicott, 1951). It seems that what I have been doing is to approach transitional experience from the standpoint of the adult world, thus entering more fully into what that form of adult experience is actually like. Let me now remind you of what Winnicott says of the baby.

The baby is hungry and has a need for the breast. He starts to *imagine* the breast and, at that moment, if the baby is lucky enough, or blessed with a good-enough mother, the mother offers her breast. Winnicott suggests that this experience allows the baby a measure of *omnipotence* in relation to the world. But if one puts it slightly differently, saying that the baby reaches out in need and discovers "out there" an object that matches or resonates to that need, then I think you will hear the echo back to what I have already said.

For Winnicott, this experience of reaching out and finding what is needed or imagined is the mainspring of creativity. It colours all future commerce with the world and determines the fate of the Self. If the experience at this stage is one of "calling" and *not* getting back an "answer", of seeking and *not* finding, the baby settles back into a compliant state: "You can't change anything, so you might as well take what comes." This, in its simplest form, is what underlies all Winnicott's theorizing about the True and False Self. When the infant at this stage has to adapt to the object excessively, the ground is laid for the development of a False Self based on compliance; but, when the *adaptive* mother predominates, *looking after the Self* by allowing herself to be created out of the baby's need, then the True Self can flourish.

In the use of the *transitional object* we can again see the baby's creativity in action, but now as an attempt to cope with the mother's diminishing adaptiveness, her response having begun to fit less closely with the baby's expectation. Put very simply: *the mother no longer provides in reality the experience the baby has been searching for, and the baby responds to this by finding it instead in the bit of blanket that lies within his reach.* In such a moment, a particular fragment of the "out there" (the bit of blanket) begins to resonate to something important "in here" (within the baby)—in other words, to that highly specific constellation of personal experience with the mother around which the core of the Self is being laid down. The baby, says Winnicott, has found/created something other than mother which helps the baby to look after himself in the mother's absence.

This moment when the baby discovers his ability to get hold of the needed experience merely by reaching into the outside world can be thought of as a kind of "Ah-ah!", or "Eureka!" (literally in Greek, "I have found it!"), experience: "Ah-ah! That's what I'm looking for! *There's* the softness, the warmth, and smell and so on . . . right here!"

Put this way, the baby is not so different from the boy or poet who reaches out to the natural world and finds there "forms" that *resonate* with his experience and support his (True) Self: "The sounding cataract haunted me like a passion" (Wordsworth, 1798). In each case, the external form and the inner subjective state somehow *recognize* each other. The subject feels *answered, comforted, soothed, supported, and responded to, and the sense of Self feels strengthened*. It is as though, to misquote Descartes just a little, the subject might say: "Someone/something out there is responding to me—therefore I am."

I am putting these words together (*resonate, recognize, answer, soothe, respond*), because they belong together, both in primitive experience and throughout our lives. In the beginning, physical *and* emotional survival depend on the presence and responsiveness of the mother; throughout our lives, *emotional* survival, the going on being of the Self, continues to depend on finding answering, resonating, recognizing responses from the outside world. *"Is there anybody there?"* This is the most basic question we can ask. What is unthinkable is for there to be no answer (this is one way of thinking about Winnicott's "unthinkable anxiety").

All this is more or less pure Winnicott, but there is something I am stressing and there may also be something I have added. I have stressed the *specificity* of the experience—the need for the answering form to fit very exactly with the inner need. What I may have added is the bit about *recognition*. The baby recognizes what it needs in the object—that much is clear. But the experience may also include the sense of *being recognized* by that which one recognizes. Prototypically, the breast (mother) recognizes the baby's need.

What I have in mind is the following: when we discover something "out there" which seems to be just what we needed, the experience is often, if not inevitably, tinged with the experience of being looked after. It is as though we feel that someone has put this thing in our way, made sure we will stumble across it. This is often quite explicitly stated by those of a religious bent, and it may be quite literally believed and acted upon by those who are psychotic and paranoid (I am thinking of the person who sees signs and messages in neutral events). So there has to be room in the feeling for a sense of someone "out there" who knows who we are and what we are about.

These two things, then, *recognition and specificity*, are closely linked together. Recognition is based on specificity—as in the recognition of face and voice and later in the recognition of all those highly specific patterns that constellate experience into the familiar and strange. Specificity is equally important in the idiosyncratic symbols we derive from our own experience and in the shared language symbols we ultimately use to designate that experience and communicate with each other about it. Recognition and specificity are thus basic to many areas of human experience, but I want to focus on one particular question: "How does the baby know that the mother recognizes him?" This question is not only basic to understanding the baby's early relatedness to his mother; it is central to every *personal* relationship in later life. To know that it is *oneself* who is recognized is crucial to the sense of identity, and it powerfully underpins our basic sense of security. How, then, does the baby know that the mother recognizes *him*?

* * *

Although we could begin to answer this question in terms of the mother's capacity to respond to her baby's instinctual needs, and although we could amplify this understanding into the *social/emotional* domain through ideas such as that of Winnicott that the mother's face is the child's first mirror (Winnicott, 1967), I want to leave all that on one side. Instead, I shall address the question by reference to a different set of ideas and concepts which have been developed from the field of empirical infant research and the direct observation of mothers and infants. I believe these ideas greatly enrich our understanding of what goes on between a mother and her baby and help us to envisage more concretely what it is that makes the interaction between them a truly personal form of relatedness.

The observations I have in mind are not closely wedded to psychoanalytic theory and, therefore, have the potential to enrich analytic theory in new ways. In addition, they are based on the observation of *non*-instinctual behaviours and so are closer to Winnicott's work on play than to older analytic writings which got stuck on instinctual gratification.

I want to refer briefly to two different sources. The first is Brazelton and Cramer's *The First Relationship* (1991); the second is Daniel Stern's *The Interpersonal World of the Infant* (1985).

First, Brazelton and Cramer. These writers summarize a great deal of research in the field of mother–infant interaction, and one of the important concepts to come out of this is that of the mother–infant *dialogue*. This covers all the different kinds of things that go on between a mother and her baby which are not immediately connected with feeding, excreting, and so on. Brazelton and Cramer discuss how such early dialogues become structured in ways that are *highly specific to each mother–infant couple*, and I want to mention just one kind of sequence as an example. The sequence in question they call *entrainment*, about which they write:

> [Infant and mother] begin to anticipate each other's responses in long sequences. Having learned each other's requirements, they can set up a rhythm as though with a set of rules. The power of this rhythm soon established an expectancy: both for the results of complying with the rhythm and for interrupting it. So powerful is this expectancy that it seems to carry each member of the dyad along. . . . Like a first violinist, one member can "entrain" the behaviour of the other by instituting a rhythm of attention and inattention which has already been established as a base for their synchrony. Their interaction thus takes on a new level of involvement. [p. 124]

The musical analogy in this description is apt because what is being described is an interaction that is structured in time, somewhat like a dance. Each partner builds on the other's moves; each learns the other's responses and in turn initiates the other into new and more complex variations. The resulting "dances", as we might call them, are unique to that couple.

If we think about separation and loss in terms of such structured sequences, it adds a new dimension to our thinking. Winnicott's transitional object (the bit of blanket, for example) can be thought of in rather concrete terms as a re-creation of aspects of the physical mother—her smell, the feel of her skin or hair, and so on. With regard to these *time*-structured sequences, however, it is more difficult to appreciate what might be salvaged or held onto by the baby if the relationship with the mother were to be broken. Such "dances" do not exist apart from the couple performing them. So if the mother is not there, who is there who can "answer" (with the expected response) when the baby "calls"?

I suspect that there are answers to this question which might lead us eventually to music and dance as art forms, but this is too large an issue to pursue here. Keeping our focus on the Self, we can remind ourselves that these sequences of response—these *entrainments*, as they are called—are part of that vital supply which the baby seeks out in the object world and which underpins his nascent sense of Self. At this stage, loss of specific supply poses a serious threat to the continuity of the True Self.

The second example I discuss is from Daniel Stern. Stern's book (1985) is a milestone in thinking about the Self, and chapter 7 of it raises fascinating ideas as to how symbolic development might arise from the unique feeling matrix of mother–infant relatedness. Stern's focus is on what he calls *attunement*. It is difficult to do justice to this concept in a few words, but I will try to give the gist. *Attunement* is concerned with the very close, perhaps almost continuous, *tracking* by the mother of her baby's affective state, or at least certain aspects of it. According to Stern, it is one root of what later becomes empathy, but distinct from it because it is an entirely non-verbal (originally pre-verbal) process. It involves the mother giving a message to her baby, in some *non-verbal* form, which conveys to the baby *the mother's participation and sharing in what the baby is feeling at that moment.*

Again, I should stress that we are not concerned here with instinctual moments and their gratification, but with what goes on between times—which is actually most of the baby's waking life—when the baby is engaging with the mother in a social way. Stern is particularly interested in the period between 9 and 15 months, which one can think of as the period preceding the development of language.

You will understand better what I mean if I give you some of Stern's examples:

> A nine month old girl becomes very excited about a toy and reaches for it. As she grabs it she lets out an exuberant "aaaah!" and looks at her mother. Her mother looks back, scrunches up her shoulders, and performs a terrific shimmy with her upper body, like a go-go dancer. The shimmy lasts only about as long as her daughter's "aaaah!" but is equally excited, joyful and intense. [p. 140]

What is important is that the mother's action echoes in its contour and duration the surge of excitement in the baby. Another example:

> A nine month old boy bangs his hand on a soft toy, at first in some anger but gradually with pleasure, exuberance and humour. He sets up a steady rhythm. Mother falls into his rhythm and says: "Kaaaa-*bam*! Kaaaa-*bam*!", the "*bam*" falling on the stroke and the "kaaaa" riding with the preparatory upswing and the suspenseful holding of his arm aloft before it falls. [p. 140]

Once again, the mother's action *echoes the pattern* of the baby's excitement. Stern thinks it very important that the mother is not strictly speaking *copying*, or mimicking, what the baby does but is *transposing some essential quality of the baby's action into another form*. This "essential quality", according to Stern, is some aspect of what the mother senses to be the baby's inner experience—its excitement, pleasure, and so on. The mother intuitively senses what it feels like being the baby at that moment and offers to the baby a kind of external rendering of that experience. In other words, she gives back to the baby *an external (sensory) representation of its immediate feeling state in a form that is syntonic and resonant with it*. As Stern says, "An attunement is a recasting, a restatement of a subjective state"(p. 161).

Stern thinks that what are responded to by the mother are not so much the discrete *categorical affects* of anger, sadness, fear, disgust, and so on, which occupy relatively little of the baby's waking life; it is, rather, "those more momentary changes in feeling states involved

in the organic processes of being alive". He calls these more momentary, more continuous changes, the *vitality affects* that we experience
"as dynamic shifts or patterned changes within ourselves or others"
(p. 156).

Unlike the categorical affects which come and go, vitality affects
are a more or less continuous background of whatever else we are
doing. They are often revealed in *how* we do things—with energy,
exuberance, interest, reluctance, heaviness, and so on. They concern a
person's state of arousal and involvement in what he is doing, and
this can change rapidly and in ways that are characteristic of the
person. The mother, therefore, can and does track her baby's vitality
affects almost continuously, and she does this in a completely intuitive way. Attunement does not involve thinking. It comes out of
being affectively involved with another person (in this case, the baby)
and is part of what we mean by being in touch with them.

Intuitive tracking or *attunement* is probably part of what we think
of as *holding or containing*; but the fact that Stern is able to describe so
precisely what he means by the term makes it a rather special concept. In my terms it is part of the specific and idiosyncratic way in
which the mother *looks after* the baby's Self.

The concept is important in a further way, as Stern points out—it
helps us to answer the question: "How does the baby, how does
anyone, begin to apprehend the nature of his own feeling states?"
And, given that feeling states are such an essential part of what we
experience as "being me", the question also concerns how we begin
to apprehend our own subjectivity, our own Self.

If we build on Stern's idea, *we can suppose that the baby begins to*
apprehend his feeling states within those forms which are first presented to
him by the mother in the shape of her attuned, intuitive responses. Just as
for Winnicott the mother's face is the child's first mirror, so, we might
suppose, these "answering forms" of the mother's attunements are
taken on board by the infant as early images or representations of
himself. Not only this—I believe that such maternal "forms" will
support and contain the infant's nascent Self in quite specific ways.
Attuned responses fit the (True) Self and are confirmatory of it. As
I put it earlier, "Someone out there is responding to me—therefore I
am".

I think there is a way from here to imagining how the baby could
begin *to look after himself* without the mediation of the mother's spon-

taneous attunements—when the mother is not there. Winnicott has traced a path from adaptive mother to transitional object in relation to the bit of blanket; in like manner, we could trace a path from the mother's attuned portrayals of the baby's aliveness to those forms and rhythms of the natural world which seemed to share some vital characteristic with those portrayals. And this takes us back to the beginning of this chapter and the idea that a person uses such forms and rhythms as a means of nourishment, communion, and support when the object is absent.

But this line of thought goes even further. It was Winnicott's genius that he sketched a broad and continuous trajectory from transitional object to the wider world of culture, religion, and art. He did not, though, fill in the details. Stern's ideas in particular help us to do this because they show us the mother *as the original source of those iconic and objective forms which both reveal and support the deepest and most alive parts of ourselves*. To get from the mother's first intuitive representations of the baby's self to the artist's, musician's, and poet's attempts to portray, in Suzanne Langer's terms (1942, 1953), "the forms of human feeling" is not really difficult. The more difficult bit is to find the bridge that starts one along that road. Once we have learned that there are forms "out there" that resonate, sing to, our deepest feelings, we are already aboard that road to art, religion, and what Winnicott calls "creative commerce with the world". This is the path of *creative* symbol-formation, which is quite different from the compliant accepting of received forms. It is the buzz of *resonance* which makes that difference. I mean by this a *felt* resonance between the form that represents and that inner experience that is being represented (I am supposing, of course, that the baby does, in fact, feel a buzz of resonance between the mother's attuned responses and his own feeling states).

Once the baby has made these first steps in creative symbol-formation, the step into language also contains creative possibilities. Words are then not just given, to be imposed on recalcitrant experience. They are there to make experience sing. They can resonate with experience and make it, and our Self, feel more alive. As Rilke (1960) says in one of the *Duino Elegies*:

> Are we, perhaps, here just for saying: House, Bridge, Foun-
> tain, Gate, Jug, Fruit-tree, Window,—possibly: Pillar, Tower?

but for *saying*, remember, oh, for such saying as never the things themselves hoped so intensely to be.

Words, in this sense, are in continuity with the mother's attuned portrayals of the baby's feeling state which enables the baby to "sing", to be more truly the Self that he already is.

In the myth of Narcissus, which is topical in current psychoanalytic writing, what I think ultimately destroyed Narcissus was not the *unreachableness* of his image in the pool. *It was the lack of that transforming quality which arises out of a passage through the Other.* Mirror images are always like this—they mock because of their sameness—if I move, the image moves too. *But nothing is added.* There is nothing in the image which says: "I recognize you and respond to you." Only a slavish identity with myself which tells me I am alone. My question to the Other, my reaching out to the Other, has failed and received the unthinkable answer.

In *attunement*, there is always transformation, never just mimicry. And I think the importance of this lies in the "otherness" of what is given back. Without otherness, we die (I mean by this that the True Self dies). What the mother gives back to the baby is certainly *similar* to what the baby gave to the mother—through this the baby knows he has been recognized and that experience has been shared. But it is also *different*, and by this the baby knows he is not alone. There is *someone* there (different and other) who is sharing experience with him.

I want to illustrate all this with some thoughts about a poem by Thomas Hardy (1979), who was obsessed by the absence and loss of loved figures. It is called "The Voice" and starts like this:

Woman much missed, how you call to me, call to me,
Saying that now you are not as you were
When you had changed from the one who was all to me,
But as at first, when our day was fair.

Note the first line: "Woman much missed, how you call to me, call to me. ..." It is an invocation to the poet's lost love, and it is something about the cadence that is important: "...how you call to me, call to me". The "caaawl", with its drawn out syllable, seems to evoke the longing and reaching out for what is lost; the repetition, with its falling cadence and lower tone, somehow creates the semblance of an answer, a response: "Woman much missed, how you call to me, call to me. . . ." The second "call to me" is more than just an echo of the first. It is different, although the words are the same. Like the attuned responses of Stern's mothers, it gives something back that was not there the first time round. The effect of this is to create a presence. This woman who is missed is somehow answering down the corridors of time and memory.

> Woman much missed, how you call to me, call to me,
> Saying that now you are not as you were
> When you had changed from the one who was all to me,
> But as at first, when our day was fair.

> Can it be you that I hear? Let me view you, then,
> Standing as when I drew near to the town
> Where you would wait for me: yes, as I knew you then,
> Even to the original air-blue gown!

Note here that the cadence of the first stanza is again repeated. The poet is listening: "Can it be you that I hear?" And then comes the answering half of the line: "let me view you, then"—echoing the answer of the first line in its rhythm and cadence, but again in a different form—the mother never just mimics, she always transposes and transforms.

And so it goes on in the third stanza as well:

> Or is it only the breeze, in its listlessness
> Travelling across the wet mead to me here
> You being ever dissolved to wan wistlessness,
> Heard no more again, far or near?

The same falling cadence is still there, but the illusion of the woman's presence created by it is beginning to dissolve: there is only the sound and rhythm of the breeze in the wet meadow. The sense of that sound as recreating or containing the presence of the woman is beginning to fail. It is as though the bit of blanket is becoming "just a bit of blanket" again.

And then the last stanza:

> Thus I; faltering forward,
>   Leaves around me falling,
> Wind oozing thin through the thorn from norward,
>   And the woman calling.

Here the rhythms are breaking up—like the illusion. A sense of weight and weariness, winter and isolation, and a final falling cadence of the woman's voice, now more absence than presence.

I think this poem illustrates how the poet's experience is recreated in the actual rhythm and cadence of the lines. It is not just that the content and the imagery say what the poet is wanting to say, which in a way they do. It is the fact that the very relationship with the woman, a kind of *dialogue* with her, is portrayed and enacted in the structure of the poem. It is the rhythms of a lost dialogue which are brought to life in the poem and these bring to the Self a feeling of the woman's presence which is at least momentarily comforting and restoring.

* * *

In this chapter I have explored in rather free fashion some of the ways in which a person may look after his (True) Self when what is needed is not forthcoming from the object.

The idea of looking after the Self is implicit in almost everything that Winnicott wrote and is closely connected with the idea of maternal responsiveness. What perhaps is not so clearly spelled out is the degree to which this responsiveness, or lack of it, actually gets into the structure of the Self. In spite of his emphasis on the primary relational unit of mother and baby ("There is no such thing as a baby"), he never, I think, quite manages to say that the Self that is formed and nurtured within this unit is itself relational in its very constitution. There is no such thing as a Self in isolation. Even when alone we are relating, as Winnicott knew—searching for that Other who, in some way, enables us to be the Self that potentially we are.

It is the centrality of the quest for an answering Other about which I have tried to say something here. The focus of object relations theory is on that which the Self does, or wants to do, to the object. By focusing on the need of the Self for recognition and answering response *from* the object, we are led into a different area of human reality in which the very possibility of being a subject (a True Self) depends on the reflections and confirmations that come from this object.

CHAPTER SIX

The Self: what is it?

Nina Coltart

S ome years ago, a patient was referred to me for assessment. She was very depressed. Thin and pale, her hair untended, she sat before me, the very essence of hopeless despair.

She was living at home and trying to keep some semblance of order there. Her three children were grown up and living away. Yes, they visited sometimes, and she wished her daughter, at least, could be with her longer, but she was busy with her own children and one couldn't blame her—or anyone else for what was happening. But she didn't think this could go on much longer.

Yet this woman was not the primary patient at all. Her state of extreme dejection mixed with rage, her exhausted pallor, her impaired appetite and sleep, with the sense of an almost total loss of the vigorous, merry person she thought she knew her Self to be, were, given the circumstances of her life, wholly appropriate. She was not *ill*. But the idiom of her sense of Self was not armed against what fate had in store for her. What was happening to this 55-year-old woman was that her 54-year-old husband had rapidly progressive Alzheimer's disease. But for what was wrong with her, there was no name, though she was depressed and even had classical symptoms. What was wrong, however, was life. She was the primary carer of someone with whom she had spent over thirty happy years with a full, demanding family life. Like many women in such circumstances, she had had neither time nor need to think about her Self. Yet now she felt that someone she knew intimately without giving much thought to the matter, that is, her Self, was lost and gone. And this was because another Self, whom she had known, if anything more intimately, and also loved, was disintegrating beside her, more irretrievably lost than she. He had disappeared into a wandering, childish stranger, who rarely knew her and would not speak with her or say her name, save, it seemed, almost by accident and forgotten a minute later.

I open with this sad story, which stands out among the many hundreds of assessments that I have done in the last thirty years, because it not only draws attention to the other sufferer, who often gets forgotten, but also speaks on many fronts to the subject of my chapter. The state of being of the wife shows something of how the Self exists not as an isolated identity, but as part of a context in which the main influences on the structure are other selves, minutely interacting with one's own Self, affecting from moment to moment one's subjective experience. But the state of her husband was even more tragic. Alterations in physiology and chemistry of his brain were steadily erasing him as a Self for others and, even more irremediably, as a Self to himself.

The study of neurology tends to involve the belief that the Self is a complex, indefinable result of living in a body, and nothing but that. Indeed, those who cannot accept anything defined by such words as "soul" or "spirit", which point to a non-physical essence, will claim evidence from such deteriorating mental conditions as I have described. Brain damage following trauma is the commonest source of adverse change in a hitherto known and loved personality, almost always for the worse; there are only occasional exceptions, as in some of those cases cited by Oliver Sacks (Sacks, 1985), where physical pathology, loss of insight, and loss of an original sense of Self can induce a good-humoured, rather than anguished, attitude to life.

In contrast to physiological damage to the Self is the bizarre phenomenon, apparently without physical foundation, and sighted more commonly in the United States than in the United Kingdom, of multiple personality disorder. Described in medical literature from early in the nineteenth century, the condition usually involves a female patient, with a psychiatric history. She begins to manifest numerous alternate personalities, which are often very unlike her primary Self and may include presentation as a male. She has the capacity to sustain up to five or six independent entities, sometimes conscious, sometimes unconscious of their co-existence. It is notable that the disorder is most commonly reported during periods when the diagnosis itself is fashionable and the therapist, therefore, more likely to be accepting. It is reported especially by practitioners with a strong interest in hypnosis and in patients with a history of childhood abuse.

In this condition, there is rarely *conscious* simulation, which, if ever attempted, is hard to sustain, as the secondary personality breaks down when conscious effort is involved. Thus, the common link with *brain pathology* is that the *unconscious* is involved in the aetiology and maintenance of the difference in Self experience, of which the patients are unaware. (And this is true of all cases subsumed under the heading of true hysteria—including fugue states and conversion symptoms.)

Attention, then, to the nature of the Self, equally in sickness as in health, points to the supremacy of the unconscious in all its mystery and to the heart of my question: "The Self: what is it?"—which is perhaps more graspable when framed as, "Yourself: who are you?" The temptation to reply, with the philosopher John Locke, that we are the sum of our memories is undermined, firstly, by the change, as I have indicated, in respect to personal identity through trauma or physical pathology, with a consequent loss of previous memories and the substitution of new ones. And, secondly, there is the question of "false memories", genuinely believed by the subject (at least for a while), and masking what Christopher Bollas alludes to as the "unthought known" (Bollas, 1987), and reaffirming the unconscious, as colonized especially by Freud, as the source of the Self and the focus of our probings.

Two of Freud's great legacies were his refusal to accept the apparent impenetrability of the unconscious with all its randomness and his development of the method of free association.

In free association, the patient, relaxed and somewhat dependent in his relationship to the analyst, is encouraged to talk, as far as possible without defences or censorship on the randomness of his material. Through such talking, and through the generative silences that are interspersed, the patient will begin to share in a process of learning. He begins to learn how to know something of his Self-experience, as what he says is attended to by the analyst's whole receptive being, which plays back to him ideas, echoes, undercurrents, and these, in turn, deepen his own Self-awareness.

This is the very stuff of psychoanalysis, where, in many an ongoing session, nothing of apparent brilliance or penetration may occur. Essentially, what we are faced with, time after time, in a psychoanalysis, is someone asking, "My Self: what is it? Who am I?" By participating in the process, the questioner appreciates that an approximation of an answer begins to appear—and that is, that there is no direct answer. Our question is an impossible one, but for that reason endlessly fascinating, not to be dismissed, but to be approached slowly, skilfully, and with care, until we begin to know aspects of ourself, to trust ways of exploring them, and to grasp the unthinkable—that the whole will always be greater than the sum of its parts. This awareness is evident in Freud's later writing, which increasingly features the term "Self" as the totality of the subjective sense of being.

But while Freud maintained a one-person psychology, one of the first great developments in analytic theory came through Guntrip, Fairbairn, and, later, Winnicott, who saw that a person is not a Self except in *relationship*. As Winnicott expressed it epigrammatically, "There is no such thing as a baby". This means that, from the beginning, we become our own individual selves only in the constant interaction of the to-ing and fro-ing between us and our mothers, which for some months is symbiotic. Since the development of increasing complexity in object relations theory, or two-person psychology, it is accepted that no Self can develop except in the intersubjective milieu of other selves continually feeding and influencing it.

This relates to another development in psychoanalysis in that many patients today are far more concerned with a search for Self than with their symptoms. In symptoms, the body is using its language as the servant of psychic events, translating, through readable symbolic equivalents, disturbances at the otherwise inaccessible levels of unconscious conflict or misery. What were originally called hysterical conversion symptoms and also psychosomatic states have in some measure been replaced, especially among the young, by demands for "space" to find their "Selves".

From a focus on the language of symbols, in symptoms and in dreams, the psychoanalytic job has shifted to providing not only a special kind of space, but also to offering hints towards exploring and developing the sense of Self, by means of skilled and/or intuitive interactions through the rapport of our own Selves with those of our analysands. Above all, we assist in the removal of fear that arises from *the failure to find a voice* for the Self and in finding "some way, often through silences, to live with the section in the library of consciousness marked 'unknown' which this word, Self, signifies" (Bollas, 1995).

For we can help the frightening sense of a loss of Self in a patient by intersubjectively reacting to the fact that *his Self has an effect on ours*, and as our patients consciously and unconsciously use us as their object, they are gradually opened to knowing this and the Self that is affecting us.

Yet as the "over-determined and cumulatively constituted internal object" (Bollas, 1987, p. 148), this Self cannot be clearly represented in thought or speech. The "I" speaks for the Self, which is better designated the "Me". The "I" is active, can think, reflect, decide, argue, and so on, but can only speak for different modes of "Me", which itself has no direct voice. We *cannot speak our Self*. The signifier and signified make up a complex whole, which is at any one time beyond our grasp. It is, rather, our *sense* of Self which is important to us. While this may be strong, it is neither definable nor stable, but constantly in process. As affirmed by Christopher Bollas (1995) in his perceptive and creative evocations of the Self in terms of "an idiom of being", in all its elusiveness:

> Self is an apparently indefinable, yet seemingly essential word—it names its *thing*, it is saturated with *it*, the indescribable is signified. . . . [p. 148]

> I believe that each of us begins life as *a peculiar but unrealized idiom of being,* and in a lifetime transforms that idiom into sensibility and personal reality. Our *idiom* is an aesthetic of being driven by an urge to articulate its theory of form by selecting and using objects so as to give them form. [p. 151]

This synthesis which is our Self can be *felt* even if it has no voice, and if we have developed our sense of Self, we sense its truth. Thus the analysand comes gradually to the realization that his Self is not a void but, at least in part, a mystery. He experiences us experiencing himself. With this, the anxiety fades away.

This dimension of mystery perhaps has greater connotations with religion than with psychoanalysis. and Freud's own opposition to religion doubtless contributed to his dedication to creating the structure of psychoanalysis, with a need, conscious or unconscious, to disprove such woolly spiritual notions as the "soul" or, indeed, God.

However, the prejudices of our founder do not preclude the existence of those analysts, amongst whom I count myself, with a religious temperament, although the combined espousal of psychoanalysis with Christianity, the religion of our culture, can be difficult to sustain. And although it was not the Freudian demon that drove me out of Christianity, which had occurred some years before my own analysis, I was still searching in the early 1960s when I embarked on my analytic training. I came across Buddhism in a fortunate stroke of my destiny in that I encountered, among Buddhists of my acquaintance, an American Theravadan monk, trained in a forest monastery in Thailand, who has subsequently been recognized as one of the great modern teachers of his way of life. This monk became my teacher.

While possessing ethical and moral similarities with other religions and strong doctrinal differences, Buddhism stands unique in the history of religious thought in its denial of the existence of a soul—or Self, which tend, in Western thought, to be treated as synonymous terms. The Self, as an autonomous entity, is an invention of the last three centuries and of the Industrial Revolution, with the far-reaching consequences of the printing press and—less obviously, perhaps—the increasingly widespread availability of mirrors. This gave to the individual a greater sense of difference, of uniqueness in this world, detracting from the given focus on eternal life for the immortal, as it were, impersonal soul, in the next world. Indeed, within secular psychoanalysis, Lacan's mirror stage—the infant's first recognition of itself in the glass—can be seen as a brief illusion of its true Self, the Me, and thereafter any ideas about the Self are less true than that core experience, the seen and realized Self.

Within many major religions, however, the focus remains on the progress and redemption of each soul, either through judgement and the threat, in the popular mind, of consignment to Heaven or Hell (as in Christianity) or through refinement, reincarnation, and ultimate union with God or Atman or the Universal Soul (as in Hinduism). Despite belief in reincarnation in some forms of Buddhism, the Buddha, inclined to keep silence when answers were likely to be metaphysically beyond his audience, on being asked if there is an eternal spirit that reincarnates, said: "All truths are without Self." This links with the Buddhist insistence that there is no superordinate supreme being: Buddhism is the ultimate paradox—an atheistic religion, whose "three Signs of Being" both counterpoint and resonate with the tenets of psychoanalysis.

These signs refer to qualities (named in Pali, the language of basic Buddhism) that apply to all living beings. Firstly, *Dukkha* or "suffering" refers not only to gross suffering like physical pain or severe grief, illness, or death, but also to all the effects of craving or attachment and might include, for example, dislike of the passing of good things or the spoiling of the present by anxious anticipation of the future. Such states are said to arise from the pain and loss inherent in natural human affections.

Secondly, *Anicca* signifies transience or impermanence and rejects the notion of an immutable soul.

Thirdly, *Anatta* means no abiding Self, for there is a theology neither of eternity nor of immortality in Buddhism. And it is this that sticks in the spiritual gullets of those with Christian backgrounds. Nowadays, having been a Buddhist for twenty-five years, this precept seems to me so intimately tied in with the first two signs of Being that I wonder how I originally found it so difficult. For it took me twelve years of daily meditation and regular listening to good teaching until one day I recognized that, unnoticed, I had "realized" its truth, quite quietly and simply, with neither striving nor strain, with scarcely a conscious thought. I had long since decided that I trusted the Buddha's teachings and the injunction: "Don't just trust me—don't take it from me—try it for yourself, see what *you* think."

This served to encourage my faith in the Buddhist process, very much as I had faith in the overall psychoanalytic process even during experiences with patients of being in darkness for long periods. I thought that if *Anatta* (no abiding Self) were fundamentally true, I would either realize it in time or I would not, and trying too hard got in the way of oneself in the process. This resembles the analytic process of coming to know, and roam more freely in, the elusive sense of Self, without ever reaching a summative point of being able to speak it or give the Me one voice.

I have alluded to these teachings because they seem to me to mesh so closely with my own remarks on the Self and its lack of some central unchanging core in its constant flux and modification, evoking paradoxically both a recognition and a strange-ness. This third Sign of Being has been described by a Buddhist monk in the following way:

> What we call "I" is a combination of physical and mental aggregates working together interdependently in a flux of momentary change within the laws of cause and effect; there is nothing permanent, everlasting, unchanging or eternal in the whole of existence.

To temper this austere vision, let me add in conclusion that Buddhism operates on two levels of language and expression, even as there are two levels of truth, which could be termed "conventional" and "ultimate". Our language reflects and determines the experience of inhabiting a world of selves, with "I" and "Me" and "Myself" and "Forever" as the existential realities that really count. This relates to my feeling of a certain ironic enjoyment that my life's work is to relate with all the care and skill my Self can give to help, rescue, repair, and build up the Selves of others. As if I *do* know clearly what I am talking about and as if the Self were accessible or speakable. It is like eating the mint with a hole, which can be very pleasurable. . . .

REFERENCES

Bion, W. (1959). "Attacks on Linking." *International Journal of Psycho-Analysis, 40.*

Bollas, C. (1987). *The Shadow of the Object.* London: Free Association Books.

Bollas, C. (1995). "What Is This Thing Called the Self?" In: *Cracking Up.* London: Routledge.

Brazelton, T., & Cramer, B. (1991). *The Earliest Relationship.* London: Karnac Books.

Chasseguet-Smirgel, J. (1987). "Wise Baby and Grandson." *Free Associations, 10,* 59.

Farhi, N. (1993). "D. W. Winnicott and a Personal Tradition." In: *From the Words of My Mouth.* London: Routledge.

Fonagy, P. (1995). "Psychoanalysis, Cognitive–Analytic Therapy, Mind and Self." *British Journal of Psychotherapy, 11.*

Fordham, F. (1967). "A Compendium of Reviews." *Journal of Analytical Psychology, 40* (3) (July 1995).

Freud, S. (1920). *Beyond the Pleasure Principle. S.E., 18.*

Freud, S. (1926). "Inhibitions, Symptoms and Anxiety." *S.E., 20.*

Greene, J. (1980). "Flash-Back." In: *Dead Man's Fall*. London: Bodley Head.

Hardy, T. (1979). "The Voice." In: *The Collected Poems*. London: Macmillan/Papermac.

Lacan, J. (1948). "Aggressivity in Psychoanalysis." In: *Ecrits. A Selection*. London: Tavistock, 1977.

Lacan, J. (1949). "The Mirror Stage." In: *Ecrits. A Selection*. London: Tavistock, 1977.

Lacan, J. (1953). "The Function and Field of Speech and Language in Psychoanalysis." In: *Ecrits. A Selection*. London: Tavistock, 1977.

Lacan, J. (1957). "The Agency of the Letter in the Unconscious or Reason since Freud." In: *Ecrits. A Selection*. London: Tavistock, 1977.

Lacan, J. (1960). "The Subversion of the Subject and the Dialectic of Desire in the Freudian Unconscious." In: *Ecrits. A Selection*. London: Tavistock, 1977.

Lacan, J. (1973). *The Four Fundamental Concepts of Psycho-Analysis*. Harmondsworth: Penguin, 1979.

Laing, R. D. (1960). *The Divided Self*. London: Tavistock.

Langer, S. (1942). *Philosophy in a New Key: A Study of the Symbolism of Reason, Rite and Art*. Cambridge, MA: Harvard University Press.

Langer, S. (1953). *Feeling and Form*. London: Routledge & Kegan Paul.

MacNeice, L. (1964). *Selected Poems*. London: Faber.

Merleau-Ponty, M. (1962). *The Phenomenology of Perception*. London: Routledge & Kegan Paul.

Phillips, A. (1988). *Winnicott*. London: Fontana.

Rilke, R. M. (1960). *Selected Works* (2 vols., trans. J. B. Leishman). London: Hogarth Press.

Roudinesco, E. (1986). *Jacques Lacan and Co. A History of Psychoanalysis in France, 1925-1985*. London: Free Association Books, 1990.

Sachs, O. (1985). *The Man Who Mistook His Wife for a Hat*. London: Duckworth.

Searles, H. (1959). "The Effort to Drive the Other Person Crazy—An Element in the Aetiology and Psychotherapy of Schizophrenia." *British Journal of Medical Psychology, 32*.

Sechehaye, M. A. (1951). *Symbolic Realization*. New York: International Universities Press.

Stern, D. N. (1985). *The Interpersonal World of the Human Infant*. New York: Basic Books.

Tustin, F. (1981). *Autistic States in Children*. London: Routledge.

Winnicott, D. W. (1945). "Primitive Emotional Development." In: *Through Paediatrics to Psychoanalysis*. London: Hogarth Press, 1975. [Reprinted London: Karnac Books, 1992.]

Winnicott, D. W. (1947). "Hate in the Countertransference." In: *Through Paediatrics to Psychoanalysis*. London: Hogarth Press, 1975. [Reprinted London: Karnac Books, 1992.]

Winnicott, D. W. (1949a). "Mind and Its Relation to the Psyche-Soma." In: *Through Paediatrics to Psychoanalysis*. London: Hogarth Press, 1975. [Reprinted London: Karnac Books, 1992.]

Winnicott, D. W. (1949b). "Ordinary Devoted Mother." In: *Babies and Their Mothers*. London: Free Association Books, 1987.

Winnicott, D. W. (1950). "Aggression in Relation to Emotional Development." In: *Through Paediatrics to Psychoanalysis*. London: Hogarth Press, 1975. [Reprinted London: Karnac Books, 1992.]

Winnicott, D. W. (1951). "Transitional Objects and Transitional Phenomena." In: *Through Paediatrics to Psychoanalysis*. London: Hogarth Press, 1975. [Reprinted London: Karnac Books, 1992.]

Winnicott, D. W. (1952). "Anxiety Associated with Insecurity." In: *Through Paediatrics to Psychoanalysis*. London: Hogarth Press, 1975. [Reprinted London: Karnac Books, 1992.]

Winnicott, D. W. (1954). "Withdrawal and Regression." In: *Psycho-Analytic Explorations*. London: Karnac Books, 1989.

Winnicott, D. W. (1956). "Primary Maternal Preoccupation." In: *Through Paediatrics to Psychoanalysis*. London: Hogarth Press, 1975. [Reprinted London: Karnac Books, 1992.]

Winnicott, D. W. (1960). "Counter-Transference." In: *The Maturational Processes and the Facilitating Environment*. London: Hogarth Press, 1965. [Reprinted London: Karnac Books, 1990.]

Winnicott, D. W. (1962). "Ego Integration in Child Development." In: *The Maturational Processes and the Facilitating Environment*. London: Hogarth Press, 1965. [Reprinted London: Karnac Books, 1990.]

Winnicott, D. W. (1963a). "Communicating and Not Communicating Leading to a Study of Certain Opposites." In: *The Maturational Processes and the Facilitating Environment*. London: Hogarth Press, 1965. [Reprinted London: Karnac Books, 1990.]

Winnicott, D. W. (1963b). "Morals and Education." In: *The Maturational Processes and the Facilitating Environment*. London: Hogarth Press, 1965. [Reprinted London: Karnac Books, 1990.]

Winnicott D. W. (1967). "Mirror-Role of Mother and Family in Child Development." In: *Playing and Reality*. London: Tavistock, 1971. [Reprinted London: Routledge, 1993.]

Winnicott, D. W. (1969). "Use of an Object and Relating through Identifications." In: *Playing and Reality*. London: Tavistock, 1971.

Winnicott, D. W. (1970). "On the Basis for Self in the Body." In: *Psycho-Analytic Explorations*. London: Karnac Books, 1989.

Winnicott, D. W. (1971a). "Creativity and Its Origins." In: *Playing and Reality*. London: Tavistock.

Winnicott, D. W. (1971b). "Dreaming, Fantasy, and Living: A Case-History Describing a Primary Dissociation." In: *Playing and Reality*. London: Tavistock, 1971.

Winnicott, D. W. (1971c). "Playing: Creative Activity and the Search for Self." In: *Playing and Reality*. London: Tavistock.

Wordsworth, W. (1798). "Lines Written a Few Miles above Tintern Abbey." In: *Selected Poems*. London: Collins, 1959.

INDEX